"I couldn't even read through the table of contents without feeling all hot and bothered. Israeli cuisine is exciting in its own right, but Danielle has just taken it to an entirely new level. "

—**MOLLY YEH,** My Name is Yeh

"Reading *Modern Israeli Cooking* made me want to strap on an apron and jump in the kitchen with Danielle, such is her passion for cooking fun, flavorful food that doesn't take itself so freakin' seriously. Though her story begins with an Israeli bent, the inspirations transcend all borders, easily captivating the most reluctant of cooks and transporting them to a place of inspiration and incredible eats."

—**NELL CASEY,** Food Editor at Gothamist

"Danielle's recipes paint a tale of time, place and people, while her way with words is as unique as it is humorous. Her methods are clear to all, and the results always deliver. You are lucky to have bought this book!"

—**AMANDA JAMES,** Publisher of Food & Travel at Pepper Passport

PAGE STREET
PUBLISHING CO.

Copyright © 2017 Danielle Oron

First published in 2015 by
Page Street Publishing Co.
27 Congress Street, Suite 105
Salem, MA 01970
www.pagestreetpublishing.com

Distributed by Macmillan, sales in Canada by The Canadian Manda Group.

21   20   19   18   17   1   2   3   4   5

ISBN-13: 978-1-62414-473-8
ISBN-10: 1-62414-473-X

Library of Congress Control Number: 2017942620

Cover design and photography by Danielle Oron
Book design by Page Street Publishing Co.

Printed and bound in China

Page Street is proud to be a member of 1% for the Planet. Members donate one percent
of their sales to one or more of the over 1,500 environmental and sustainability charities
across the globe who participate in this program.

DANIELLE ORON
FOUNDER OF THE BLOG I WILL NOT EAT OYSTERS

MODERN ISRAELI COOKING

100 NEW RECIPES FOR TRADITIONAL CLASSICS

PAGE STREET
PUBLISHING CO.

CONTENTS

BEACH / 61

SLOW COOKING / 85

BRUNCH / 107

SWEETS / 185

STAPLES / 211

INTRODUCTION

It's very hard to pinpoint what Israeli cuisine is, exactly. Israel is a melting pot of several cultures that migrated to what was once called Palestine. Many ethnicities influence the cuisine you'll find there today, including Moroccan, Eastern European, Yemeni, Egyptian, Iraqi and Turkish. So when I use the term *Israeli cooking*, it doesn't necessarily mean it was born in the state of Israel, it means that you can find it there now. It's a combination of old-world and new-world cuisines.

My family moved from Tel Aviv to New Jersey when I was just three. As much as I tried to fit in, my family was always referred to as "those crazy Israelis," in the best way possible. We are loud, occasionally obnoxious, compassionate, inviting, caring and warm. Israeli cooking is very similar: bold, in your face and full of love.

Israelis eat a lot of their meals family-style with tons of side plates filled with salads and dips, and almost always with a carb. Mmm. Carbs. This is a culture whose focal point is eating and feeding. My dad would come home very late each weekend from his army outpost, and his mom would be at the door with a plate of food before he could even ask if there was something to eat. There are more Israeli cooking shows than there are American ones. Shocking, I know. Life is centered around the kitchen table. When you invite someone into your home, whether you know them or not, you bring them to the table, not the couch. I hope that these feelings of love and sharing are conveyed through these dishes.

I am infatuated with food. I was a food-obsessed child who asked my mom what we were having for dinner while we were eating breakfast and am now an adult who plans dinners for months in advance. You should see my Pinterest account!

These recipes combine my culinary background in French technique with classic Israeli flavors to create new and modern dishes. They are not kosher in any sense of the word. They've got a very American-Israeli feel to them, which reflects who I am. . . . I guess that would make sense—just had a eureka moment there. My recipes are very much like what Israeli food has come to be; a combination of old and new.

I will ask only that you invite some friends over and share this food with them. And even if you don't, I won't really know so . . . #dowhatiwant!

WEEKDAYS

EVERYDAY KIND OF FOOD

There is a particular type of love that goes into weekday meals. It's not the pour-heart-and-soul-into-every-morsel-of-this-food kind of love, but more of a nourishing love—the kind of love that comes from a mother who's trying to fatten up her kids and make sure they don't *ever* go hungry. In our Israeli-American home, these meals normally were eaten right after my brother and I came home from school. My mom took the time to make sure we always had a hearty dish of something waiting for us just as we walked in the door. Don't get me wrong: There were those days where she slapped tomato paste, cheese, oregano and olives onto half a pita and called it "Pizza Night." Even then, there would be that love in it: nourishing love.

These weekday meals are meant to fill you up. I've taken some of my mother's usual-suspect recipes and tuned them up with a modern touch. She would make basic schnitzel and serve it with a bit of Israeli salad. But I have taken it to another level by making it like a fried-chicken sandwich with tons of slaw and pickles. They're not *quick* recipes, like you'll find in some cookbooks, but that extra few minutes you spend on dinner will pay off in the depth of flavor. For example: "In 30 minutes, you can get this on the table!" I believe that you should put in a bit of effort to create a meal that looks and tastes beautiful. So make extra to bring to work the next day. You go and show off!

CHICKEN SHAWARMA RICE BOWL WITH QUICK-PICKLED TOMATOES

TAKE THE MYSTERY OUT OF STREET MEAT

In Tel Aviv, shawarma is everywhere, and each place makes it slightly different. Layers of chicken, lamb, beef or a combo of meats are stacked on a large rotating spit that slowly grills it all day. Best part: all the toppings and sauces that you can put on it. I've adapted the classic street food for the home kitchen. The deliciously spiced chicken is cut thin to mimic the "shaved" effect of the meat you get from the vendor. Quick-pickled tomatoes give the dish a tangy burst of freshness. If you like things a bit spicy, serve this with a little harissa.

MAKES 4 SERVINGS

INGREDIENTS

SHAWARMA

1 ½ lb (680 g) boneless skinless chicken thighs

1 ½ tbsp (10 g) ground cumin

2 tsp (4 g) ground turmeric

1 ½ tsp (3 g) ground coriander

1 ½ tsp (3 g) paprika

1 ½ tsp (3 g) garlic powder

1 tsp freshly ground black pepper

¼ tsp hot paprika

⅛ tsp cinnamon

⅛ tsp cloves

1 tsp salt

3 tbsp (45 ml) olive oil

ONION RICE

1 tbsp (15 ml) olive oil

1 small yellow onion, diced

1 cup (195 g) basmati rice, rinsed

2 cups (480 ml) water

1 ½ tbsp (11 g) consommé powder

¼ tsp salt

Fresh pepper to taste

QUICK-PICKLED TOMATOES

3 Roma tomatoes, cut into 1-inch (2.5-cm) cubes

¼ cup (26 g) sliced red onions

1 tbsp (3 g) chopped cilantro

¾ cup (180 ml) water

⅓ cup (80 ml) white vinegar

1 ½ tsp (9 g) salt

1 ½ tsp (7 g) sugar

1 ½ tbsp (23 ml) olive oil, for frying

Tahini, to taste (page 212)

Harissa, optional (page 215)

METHOD

Clean the chicken by trimming off any skin, fat or cartilage. Pound the thighs out flat using a mallet or just the heel of your hand. Slice them into thin long strips, about ¼ inch (6.5 mm) thick. The thinner, the better!

Combine the cumin, turmeric, coriander, paprika, garlic powder, pepper, hot paprika, cinnamon, cloves, salt and olive oil in a large bowl to form a paste. Transfer the sliced thighs to the bowl and massage the paste into the chicken. Cover and refrigerate for at least 30 minutes. Can be made the day before and left in the fridge overnight.

To make the rice, heat the 1 tablespoon (15 ml) of oil over medium heat in a medium saucepot. Sauté the onion until they're translucent, about 3 minutes. Add the rice. Stir and cook for a minute until the rice is fragrant and slightly translucent. Stir in the water, consommé powder, salt and some fresh pepper to taste. Bring the water to a boil, cover the pot and simmer for 20 minutes.

While the rice is cooking, make the quick-pickled tomatoes. In a nonreactive bowl, combine the tomatoes, red onions and cilantro. In a small pot over medium heat, bring the water, vinegar, salt and sugar to a light simmer. Once the salt and sugar have dissolved, remove the liquid from the heat and pour it over the tomatoes. Let marinate for about 15 minutes.

Heat 1 ½ tablespoons (23 ml) of olive oil in a large frying pan over medium heat. Working in batches, without crowding, add the chicken to the pan in one layer. Cook for 2–3 minutes on each side until golden brown and crispy around the edges. Don't move them around the pan, just flip the strips once! This will ensure you get a nice crust on the chicken. Save the oil from the pan to drizzle over the top of the rice, if you're that kind of person. I sure am.

Plate the dish by spooning some rice into each of the serving bowls. Top with the chicken shawarma and some of the pickled tomatoes along with their juice, and drizzle some, or a lot, of tahini over top. To kick it up, add a bit of harissa to the mix.

SCHNITZEL & SUMAC SLAW SANDWICHES

THE PERFECT FRIED-CHICKEN SANDWICH

Schnitzel was something my mom made every week. Israeli schnitzel is most always made with thinly pounded chicken that is coated in breading and then pan-fried. Every child growing up in an Israeli home had this at least once a week without fail. My mom can basically make it in her sleep. Hers is particularly delicious, though. I am sharing with you my mom's classified info for the best schnitzel (She hasn't exactly approved. Well, I haven't *really* told her I'm handing out her secrets.): Dijon mustard in the egg wash plus panko mixed into the bread crumbs. Boom! I did it. Sorry, Mom.

Normally, schnitzel is served on a platter with Israeli salad and rice or mashed potatoes. I've taken the basic schnitzel and sammie-fied it. This is my Israeli take on a fried-chicken sandwich. Feel free to double up on the schnitzel and double stack it for an extra-large bad boy. The chicken is super crispy and juicy. The slaw adds the perfect amount of zing and freshness to the sandwich. If you can find Israeli pickles, that's best for the flavor combination. And don't you dare skimp on that mayo.

MAKES 4 SERVINGS

INGREDIENTS

SUMAC SLAW

2 cups (200 g) finely shredded cabbage

1 cup (100 g) finely shredded purple cabbage

½ cup (50 g) shredded carrot

¼ cup (6 g) roughly chopped cilantro

¼ cup (63 g) full-fat mayonnaise

2 tbsp (30 ml) apple cider vinegar

1 tbsp (15 ml) honey

1 tsp sumac

1 tsp salt

¼ tsp fresh black pepper

SCHNITZEL

2 skinless boneless chicken breasts

Salt for seasoning

½ cup (65 g) all-purpose flour

2 large eggs

1 ½ (27 g) tbsp Dijon mustard

⅔ cup (70 g) plain bread crumbs

⅔ cup (40 g) panko bread crumbs

1 tsp (3 g) sesame seeds

1 tsp (6 g) salt

¼ tsp fresh black pepper

Canola oil for frying

Ciabatta, cut into 4 and sliced open

Mayonnaise

Israeli pickles or kosher dill pickles, sliced

METHOD

Combine the cabbages, carrots and cilantro in a large bowl. In a small bowl, whisk together the mayonnaise, vinegar, honey, sumac, salt and pepper. Pour the dressing over the cabbage mixture and toss to coat. Set this in the fridge until ready to construct the sandwiches.

Slice each chicken breast into two pieces lengthwise as if you were butterflying the breast open, but just cut through. Pound each piece between 2 pieces of parchment paper as thin as possible using a mallet or the heel of your hand. Each piece should be about ½ inch (12 mm) thick. Season both sides with a generous amount of salt.

Prepare the breading station in baking pans or shallow bowls. In the first, place the flour. In the second, whisk together the eggs and mustard. In the last, combine the plain bread crumbs, panko, sesame seeds, salt and pepper.

Heat a large skillet with ⅓ inch (8.5 cm) of canola oil over medium heat. Once the oil is hot and rippling, dredge the chicken in the flour, shake off the excess, dip it into the egg wash, let the excess drip off and then place it into the bread crumb mixture. I press the bread crumbs into the chicken with the heel of my hand to ensure it sticks well. Place the breaded breast straight into the oil. Continue with the rest of the chicken. I can normally fit two breast fillets in the skillet at a time. Don't bread the chicken until just before you place it in the hot oil to ensure that it won't get soggy. Fry for 3 minutes on each side or until it's golden brown. Transfer onto a cooling rack. Season them with salt immediately.

Construct the sandwiches by smearing a very good amount of mayonnaise on both sides of the ciabatta. Place the schnitzel on the bread and top with the sumac slaw and pickles.

SPINACH FALAFEL

WITH GREEN TAHINI & SAUERKRAUT

Falafel: a deep-fried spiced chickpea "meatball." It's another one of those traditional Israeli street foods that you can't go a month without having. It's crispy on the outside, soft on the inside and belongs in a pita (this is my passionate belief). Green tahini is simply tahini that's mixed with an insane amount of chopped parsley to give it that green hue and herby flavor. To continue with the green theme, I added spinach to the falafel for some added vitamin K. The children will never know it's in there. . . .

MAKES 4 SERVINGS

INGREDIENTS

SPINACH FALAFEL

4 cups (160 g) spinach

1 (15 oz [425 g]) can chickpeas, drained and rinsed*

1 tbsp (1.5 g) chopped cilantro

2 cloves garlic

½ tbsp (4 g) cumin

½ tsp salt

1 tbsp (8 g) all-purpose flour

¼ tsp baking powder

GREEN TAHINI

1 recipe Tahini (page 212)

1 ½ cups (36 g) chopped parsley

Canola oil for frying

Pita, optional, but come on!

Sauerkraut

It is important to rinse the chickpeas. If you don't, the falafel has the potential to fall apart during the frying.

METHOD

Pulse the spinach in a food processor until coarsely chopped. Add the chickpeas, cilantro, garlic, cumin, salt, flour and baking powder. Pulse until all the ingredients are finely chopped but not pureed into hummus. Place the mixture in a bowl and set in the fridge for 15 minutes.

While the falafel mix rests in the fridge, make the tahini by adding 1 ½ cups (36 g) of chopped parsley to the basic tahini recipe.

Roll the falafel into 14–16 balls. Flatten the tops and bottoms a little bit for easy frying.

Heat a large frying pan with ¼ inch (6 mm) of oil over low heat. Once the oil is rippling, fry the falafel in batches until golden brown, about 1 to 1 ½ minutes per side. Don't crowd the pan. Transfer onto a cooling rack from the oil and season with salt.

Serve inside a pita with a generous amount of sauerkraut and green tahini.

MIDDLE EASTERN BEEF FRIED RICE

BECAUSE—FRIED RICE.

Fried rice is one of the easiest things to make. It's also freaking delicious. Since rice is such a huge part of the both Chinese and Israeli cuisine, it was easy to fuse the two together. This one is made using some classic Middle Eastern spices. It comes together in no time and is perfect for a fast weeknight meal, which turns into a work lunch the following day.

MAKES 4 SERVINGS

INGREDIENTS

2 tbsp (30 ml) canola oil

1 large yellow onion, chopped

1 lb (454 g) ground beef chuck

1 tsp cumin

1 ½ tsp (3 g) paprika

1 tsp salt

¼ tsp fresh black pepper

2 large eggs

1 ½ cups (300 g) cooked basmati rice

½ cup (75 g) frozen peas

¼ cup (6 g) roughly chopped cilantro

METHOD

Heat the oil over medium-high heat in a wok or large skillet. Add the onion and sauté for 5 to 6 minutes until the onion is softened and browning. Add the beef to the wok and break it up as it browns. Mix in the cumin, paprika, salt and pepper. Stir until the beef has cooked through, about 5 minutes. Make a well in the middle of the beef and crack the eggs into the center of that well. Whisk the eggs while they cook to scramble them. Don't incorporate any of the beef until the eggs are almost completely cooked through, about 2 minutes. Mix in the rice and frozen peas. Once it's all warmed through and combined, about a minute, turn the heat off and mix in the chopped cilantro.

LENTIL & KALE HARIRA SOUP

THICK, FILLING AND LEMONY DELICIOUSNESS

Harira is a thick Moroccan soup made with lentils and chickpeas, and it's seasoned with a ton of lemon juice. Usually it's made with rice, but I remember my grandmother making it with those tiny thin vermicelli noodles—the ones you find in chicken soups and such. Feel free to switch out the noodles for rice if you'd like to make this gluten-free. I've decided that it needed kale for some extra green-power goodness. It also adds more heftiness to the soup . . . like it needs it! So comforting.

MAKES 6 SERVINGS

INGREDIENTS

1 large yellow onion

6 stalks celery

1 ½ tbsp (23 ml) olive oil

1 (15 oz [425 g]) can chickpeas, drained

1 cup (200 g) green lentils, rinsed and picked through

1 ½ tsp (3 g) turmeric

1 tsp (6 g) salt

½ tsp cumin

¼ tsp ground white pepper

½ cup (12 g) chopped parsley

½ cup (12 g) chopped cilantro

½ cup (85 g) short vermicelli noodles

2 cups (130 g) chopped kale

⅓ cup (80 ml) fresh lemon juice

Salt and fresh pepper to taste

Chopped cilantro

Labane (page 219) or sour cream

Sumac

Lemon wedges

METHOD

Grate the onion and the celery stalks in a food processor with grate attachment or by hand on the side of a box grater with the large holes.

Heat the oil in a large pot over medium heat. Add the grated celery and onion and sauté for about 4 minutes until softened and some of the liquid has evaporated. Stir in the chickpeas, lentils, turmeric, salt, cumin, white pepper, parsley and cilantro. Cook and stir for a minute to release the flavor from the spices.

Cover with 6 cups (1.5 L) of water. Turn the heat up to high and bring to a boil. Once boiling, turn the heat down to low, cover the pot and simmer for 30 minutes, stirring often.

Stir in the noodles and kale and continue cooking uncovered for another 5 minutes. Once the noodles are cooked through, turn the heat off and mix in the lemon juice. Taste for seasoning and adjust with salt and pepper.

Serve with chopped cilantro, a dollop of labane, a sprinkle of sumac and a lemon wedge.

KOFTA KEBAB FREEKEH SALAD WITH TAHINI DRESSING

MEAT IS HOW YOU WIN FRIENDS WITH SALAD

You don't win friends with salad! Right, Homer Simpson? Wrong, Homer Simpson! You definitely can with this salad. I mean . . . it's got meat! The meat here is *kofta* kebabs, which are essentially long meatballs wrapped around a skewer and grilled. You can find them in any *steakiat*, which are as prevalent as diners in the state of New Jersey, except *steakiats* contain delicious meats grilled over open flames. *Freekeh* is an ancient grain used all over the Middle East. A salad is a great way to feature it. This salad should make it to your next backyard BBQ.

MAKES 6 SERVINGS

INGREDIENTS

KOFTA KEBABS

1 large yellow onion
1 ½ lb (680 g) ground beef chuck
¼ lb (113 g) ground lamb
2 tbsp (6 g) chopped cilantro
1 tbsp (1.5 g) chopped parsley
1 tbsp (15 ml) olive oil
1 ¼ tsp (7 g) salt
½ tsp cumin
½ tsp paprika
¼ tsp fresh black pepper
¼ tsp baking powder
Pinch of allspice

TAHINI DRESSING

¾ cup (180 ml) sesame paste
2 cloves garlic, minced
2 ½ tbsp (38 ml) fresh lemon juice
½ cup (120 ml) water
½ tsp (3 g) salt

FREEKEH SALAD

1 cup (190 g) freekeh
¼ cup (26 g) sliced red onions
⅔ cup (100 g) dried cherries
½ cup (12 g) chopped parsley
4 radishes, julienned
3 tsp (6 g) sumac
Salt and pepper to taste

METHOD

Grate the onion in food processor with grate attachment or by hand on the large-hole side of a box grater. In a large bowl, mix the grated onion, beef, lamb, cilantro, parsley, olive oil, salt, cumin, paprika, pepper, baking powder and allspice until just combined. Don't overmix this! Shape the kebabs into 4-inch (10-cm)-long torpedo shapes. Should make 12–14 kebabs. You can skewer them if you like. This can be made a day ahead. Set in the fridge covered until ready to grill.

To make the tahini dressing, whisk together the sesame paste, garlic, lemon juice, water and salt. You must keep whisking if you see it separate. It will eventually come together. If it seems too thick, add an additional tablespoon (15 ml) of water and whisk again. Set aside.

To make the salad, bring a large pot of water to a boil. Add the freekeh and cook until al dente—can take anywhere between 20 and 30 minutes depending on the kind of freekeh. Drain when it's ready and set aside to cool completely. Combine the cooled freekeh with the red onions, cherries, parsley, radishes and sumac. Set aside.

Grill the kebabs by heating a grill or grill pan over medium heat. If using an indoor grill pan, use a bit of oil to prevent the kebabs from sticking. Grill the kebabs for about 3 minutes on each side until cooked through but still juicy.

Toss the salad with ½ cup (120 ml) of the tahini dressing and season with salt and pepper to taste. Serve the kebabs on top or beside the salad with the remaining dressing drizzled on top or on the side.

ZA'ATAR CHICKEN WITH PTITIM & ONION PAN SAUCE

LOOKS FANCY, HUH?

For a quick-fix dinner, there was always a spiced chicken "steak" with *ptitim* and Israeli salad in the household I grew up in. Ptitim are tiny round pastas. In the States, they're called Israeli couscous. They're fun to eat and easy as pie to make. Kids adore them. Does that make me a kid? Maybe. I wouldn't argue that. This version is a bit fancier with a gorgeous onion pan sauce. It's still a quick-fix dinner—it sounds harder than it actually is.

MAKES 4 SERVINGS

INGREDIENTS

PTITIM

2 tbsp (28 g) unsalted butter

2 cups (300 g) ptitim or Israeli couscous

2 ½ cups (600 ml) water

½ tsp salt

Fresh black pepper

ZA'ATAR CHICKEN AND SAUCE

2 boneless skinless chicken breasts

Salt for seasoning

2 tbsp (15 g) za'atar

1 tbsp (15 ml) olive oil

1 tbsp (14 g) unsalted butter

1 large yellow onion, cut into ¼-inch (6-mm) slices

1 tbsp (8 g) all-purpose flour

1 ½ cups (360 ml) chicken stock

Salt and fresh black pepper to taste

Chopped parsley

METHOD

Heat the butter over medium heat in a pot with a tight-fitting lid. Once it has melted, add the ptitim and sauté for a minute until fragrant. Cover with water and season with salt and pepper. Bring to a boil, turn the heat down to low, cover and simmer for 12 minutes.

Slice each chicken breast into two pieces lengthwise as if you were butterflying the breast open, but just cut through. Pound each piece between 2 pieces of parchment paper as thin as possible. Should be between ½ inch to ¾ inch (12 mm–19 mm) using a mallet or the heel of your hand. Season both sides with a generous amount of salt and the za'atar.

Heat the olive oil in a large skillet over medium heat. When it's hot, add the chicken. Cook for 4 minutes on each side until browned and cooked through. Remove the chicken from the pan. Add the butter and the onion. Sauté for 6–7 minutes, tossing often until the onion begins to pick up some color. Season with a pinch of salt. Sprinkle the flour over the onions and cook for about a minute to eliminate the floury flavor. Deglaze the pan with the stock, scraping the bottom to release any flavor bits. Turn the heat up to high and bring to a boil. Reduce until thickened. Season with salt and pepper to taste. Return the chicken to the pan and spoon the sauce over the top.

Place the ptitim onto each plate, top with a piece of chicken breast, onions and sauce. Garnish with chopped parsley.

UNSTUFFED CABBAGE ROLLS

SIMPLIFYING THE SIMPLE BUT MAKING IT TASTY, OBVIOUSLY

Making cabbage rolls is labor intensive. You have to peel the leaves off of the cabbage, boil them, make the stuffing, stuff the leaves, roll them, make the sauce . . . bah. No thanks. I've simplified this classic recipe to be fast, painless and dare I say, even more delicious than its original while keeping its humbleness. When I told my mom I was topping this with labane, a strained tangy yogurt, and adding white balsamic vinegar for a pop of flavor, she almost died. "But that's not how it's done. . . ." Exactly, Mom. Exactly.

MAKES 4 SERVINGS

INGREDIENTS

2 tbsp (30 ml) olive oil

1 large onion, chopped

1 lb (454 g) ground beef chuck

1 tsp salt

¼ tsp fresh black pepper

⅔ cup (130 g) basmati rice, rinsed

1 head cabbage, stem removed, roughly chopped

2 cups (480 ml) canned tomato sauce

2 cups (480 ml) water

2 tbsp (30 ml) white balsamic vinegar

Labane (page 219), or store bought

Fresh black pepper

Chopped parsley

METHOD

Heat the olive oil in a large pot with a tight-fitting lid over medium-high heat. Add the onion and sauté for 4 minutes until softened. Add the ground beef and break it up while it browns, about 5 minutes. Season with the salt and pepper. Stir in the rice and the cabbage. Add the tomato sauce and water. It should just about cover what's in the pot.

Bring it to a boil, turn the heat down to low, cover and simmer for 30–35 minutes, stirring once or twice toward the beginning of the cooking process. I like leaving the contents at the bottom of the pot untouched. Toward the end of cooking, it picks up a little color and flavor. Turn the heat off and mix in the vinegar and check for seasoning. Adjust with salt if needed.

Top each of the servings with a dollop of labane, fresh black pepper and chopped parsley.

SPICED FAVA BEAN SANDWICH

PERFECT FOR A LIGHT SPRING DINNER

Favas are constantly used in Middle Eastern cuisine. They're hearty as hell. Moroccans use them to make a dip sort of like hummus. I've taken more of the Egyptian route by cooking and mashing them with some spices. There is also a slow-cooking method in preparing favas that involves braising them in a tomato sauce. I wanted this dish to be bright, light and colorful . . . and a sandwich. Naturally. The components of this dish can also be deconstructed for an appetizer platter. And it's perfect for a picnic since this can be eaten at room temp.

MAKES 4 SERVINGS

INGREDIENTS

2 tbsp (30 ml) olive oil

3 cloves garlic, minced

1 tsp paprika

½ tsp cumin

½ tsp coriander

Pinch hot paprika

2 ½ (425 g) cups fresh or frozen fava beans, shelled

½ tsp salt

3 tbsp (45 ml) fresh lemon juice

2 tbsp (3 g) chopped cilantro

1 ½ tbsp (2 g) chopped mint

1 loaf sourdough or ciabatta

Olive oil

Salt and fresh black pepper

Labane (page 219), or store bought

2 radishes, sliced ⅟₁₆-inch (1.5-mm) thick with a mandoline

¼ fennel bulb, sliced thinly with a mandoline

Maldon salt and fresh black pepper

METHOD

Heat the olive oil in a large sauté pan over medium-low heat. Add the garlic, paprika, cumin, coriander and hot paprika. Sauté for a minute until fragrant and the oils from the spices are released. Add in the fava beans and season with salt. Toss and cook for 2 minutes. Turn the heat off and let cool slightly.

Transfer half of the fava bean mixture into a food processor. Pulse until coarsely chopped. Place the chopped and whole fava beans in a large bowl. Mix in the lemon juice, cilantro and mint. Taste and adjust the seasoning as needed.

Slice the loaf in half lengthwise. Cut off the crusted top portion of the top of the loaf for better toasting while on the grill. Heat a grill or grill pan over high heat. Drizzle both sides of the loaf halves with a very generous amount of olive oil, and season with salt and fresh black pepper. Grill each side for 1–2 minutes until charred and toasty.

Spread a good amount of labane on both halves of the toasted bread. Layer the radish, fennel and fava beans into the sandwich. Season with Maldon or other sea salt and black pepper.

CHEESY KALE PASHTIDA

YAY! PIE FOR DINNER!

A *pashtida* is like a kugel—a noodle casserole—except that it's almost always savory. This ain't your *bubbe's* sweet cinnamon kugel. I take this glorious opportunity to clear out the fridge of whatever is about to expire. You also don't need to use these specific cheeses. It's a use-what-ya-got typa thang.

MAKES 4 SERVINGS

INGREDIENTS

4 cups (250 g) short wide egg noodles

2 cups (130 g) chopped kale

5 large eggs

¼ cup (60 ml) milk

1 cup (113 g) shredded *kashkaval* or provolone cheese

1 cup (110 g) crumbled Bulgarian feta cheese

½ cup (125 g) smooth ricotta cheese

Salt and fresh black pepper to taste

1 tbsp (15 ml) olive oil

METHOD

Preheat the oven to 350°F (175°C).

Bring a large pot of salted water to a boil. Stir in the egg noodles and return to a boil. Just before the noodles are cooked through, add the chopped kale to the water. Cook for another minute and drain into a colander. Run cold water over the kale and noodles to stop the cooking.

In a large bowl, whisk the eggs and milk together until homogenous. Add the kashkaval, feta and ricotta cheese and stir. Season the mixture with salt and fresh black pepper to taste. Stir in the noodles and kale.

Heat the olive oil in a large ovenproof skillet over high heat. Once the skillet is hot, pour in the noodle mixture and spread it to the edges of the skillet. Immediately move the skillet into the oven and bake for 25 minutes. Turn the oven onto broil for 3-4 minutes to crisp and brown the top of the pashtida.

Slide it off onto a cutting board or tray and cut it like a pie.

GRILLED ENTRECOTE WITH OLIVE & BAHARAT COMPOUND BUTTER

STEAK AND BUTTER. THAT IS ALL.

Baharat is a traditional spice mix used to season meat dishes. Using it in a compound butter for steak was, I believe, a pretty brilliant idea. The olives give a nice punch to the butter and enhance the seasoning. This would be great on any steak, so use your favorite cut.

MAKES 4 SERVINGS

INGREDIENTS

5 tbsp (70 g) room-temperature unsalted butter

1 clove garlic, minced

2 tbsp (22 g) roughly chopped kalamata olives

¼ tsp salt

¼ tsp cumin

¼ tsp coriander

⅛ tsp fresh black pepper

⅛ tsp cardamom

⅛ tsp paprika

Pinch of cinnamon

Pinch of nutmeg

4 good-quality sirloin steaks

Olive oil

Salt and fresh black pepper

METHOD

Combine the softened butter with the garlic, olives, salt, cumin, coriander, pepper, cardamom, paprika, cinnamon and nutmeg. Transfer the butter onto parchment paper and roll into a tight log. Chill for 2 hours in the fridge, or 30 minutes in the freezer if you're impatient.

Prepare a baking sheet with a cooling rack on top of it and set aside. Heat a grill or grill pan over high heat. Brush both sides of the steaks with olive oil and season extra generously with salt and fresh black pepper. Grill for 4–5 minutes on one side then flip and grill for an additional 4–5 minutes for medium-rare, or 7–8 minutes for medium doneness. Please don't cook any more than that! But if you must, grill 8–10 minutes on the second side for well done.

Remove steaks onto the cooling rack. Immediately place a slice of compound butter onto each steak, lightly tent with tinfoil and let them rest for at least 5 minutes before serving. Serve extra compound butter on the side.

SPINACH & FETA HAND PIES

LIKE A SAVORY POP TART, ONLY ARTISANAL AND WAY TASTIER

Store-bought pie dough is not just for pies! These are a fun handheld dinner that kids and adults alike seem to really enjoy. They can be made ahead, frozen and baked whenever you want. Feta and spinach seemed like the right combination for them since it reminded me so much of a spinach *boureka*. They're so flaky and cheesy.

MAKES 4–5 SERVINGS

INGREDIENTS

1 tbsp (15 ml) olive oil

10 oz (283 g) spinach

1 large egg

1 (1 lb [454 g]) package frozen pie dough, thawed in the fridge

Flour for work surface

⅓ cup (37 g) crumbled Bulgarian feta cheese

Sesame seeds

Black sesame seeds

Maldon salt

METHOD

Prepare a cheesecloth-lined strainer over a bowl. Heat the oil in a large sauté pan over medium-low heat. Add the spinach and toss often as it wilts. This should take about 5 minutes. Transfer the spinach into the strainer and let it drain and come to room temperature.

Using the cheesecloth, wring out as much of the liquid from the spinach as possible and set aside.

Preheat the oven to 425°F (220°C). Prepare 2 baking sheets by lining them with parchment paper. Make the egg wash by whisking the egg with a splash of water in a small bowl.

Unroll the pie dough onto a lightly floured work surface. Roll it out a bit until it is about ¼-inch (6-mm) thick. Cut it into 4-inch (10-cm) by 3-inch (7.5-cm) rectangles. Transfer the bottom pie rectangles of each of the pies to the 2 prepared baking sheets. Top each one with 1 ½ tablespoons (15 g) of spinach and ½ tablespoon (3.5 g) of crumbled feta cheese, leaving a ½-inch (12-mm) border around the edges. Brush all 4 edges of each pie with the egg wash. Top with the other pie rectangle pressing firmly around the edges. Crimp the edges by pressing down on them with a fork. Prick a few holes along the top of each pie. Brush the tops with the egg wash and sprinkle with plain and black sesame seeds and Maldon sea salt.

At this point you can wrap and freeze the baking sheets until you would like to bake the pies. Otherwise bake for 12–14 minutes until golden brown and flaky. If baking from frozen, it can take up to 18 minutes.

FRIDAYS

SPECIAL DISHES MADE ON
SHABBAT OR HOLIDAYS

The smell in the air changes in Israel as soon as dusk hits on a Friday night. The Sabbath comes in and the mood becomes instantly lighter. Family and friends get together for a delicious and comforting dinner. It's so unique that it's very difficult to describe. It's a feeling; no words necessary. Now I'm getting all poetic on you. For me, it's not about the religious meaning of Shabbat, but the nostalgia of having family get together. At present, we live in different parts of the country and it's impossible to replicate that feeling on Friday evenings. I look forward to those rare occasions when we actually do get together. These recipes are ones that my family has made over the years for Shabbat dinners and other holidays, only a hell of a lot spunkier. Because I like spunk.

EVERYTHING CHALLAH
THE SCENT OF SHABBAT

When you walk into a home on a Friday and you smell this sweet, yeasty, warming scent of bread baking, you know it's Shabbat. Nothing smells of a Friday evening or holiday more than this one. Challah is traditional Jewish bread made with enriched dough (that just means it has eggs in it). It's very similar to brioche dough except that there is no butter in it for kosher reasons. In my family, we would tear away at it, *never* taking a knife to that shiny crust. And more often than not, it would be my dad and I who would take it down. If, by chance, there was some left over, we would save it for the Saturday morning *shakshuka*. Traditionally, sesame seeds are sprinkled over the loaf before it goes in the oven to bake. I thought . . . why not make it taste like an everything bagel? Yum.

MAKES 1 LOAF

INGREDIENTS

¾ cup (180 ml) warm water

1 ½ tbsp (18 g) sugar

¾ oz (21 g) dry active yeast, one packet

1 cup (140 g) bread flour, divided

3 ¼ cups (420 g) all-purpose flour

1 tbsp (15 ml) honey

¼ cup plus 1 tbsp (75 ml) olive oil

2 large eggs

1 egg yolk

1 ½ tsp (9 g) salt

1 large egg

1 tbsp (9 g) poppy seeds

1 tbsp (9 g) sesame seeds

1 tbsp (9 g) dried garlic flakes

1 tbsp (9 g) dried onion flakes

1 tbsp (9 g) Maldon salt

METHOD

In the bowl of an electric mixer, whisk together the warm water, sugar and yeast. Mix in half (70 g) of the bread flour, cover with a kitchen towel and let the "mother" rest in a warm spot in the kitchen for at least 1 hour.

Add the remaining bread flour, all-purpose flour, honey, olive oil, eggs, yolk and salt to the "mother" mixture. Using the dough hook attachment, mix on low for 3 minutes until the dough comes together. Turn the mixer up to medium-high and let the mixer do the kneading work for 2 more minutes.

Remove the dough from the mixer bowl and shape it into a tight round ball and place it in an oiled bowl. Cover with a kitchen towel and place it back in that warm spot. Let it rise for 2 hours. It should double in size.

Section off the dough into 3 or 6 equal balls and roll them into strands. Braid the challah with 3 or 6 strands and transfer it to a greased baking sheet.

Whisk an egg with a splash of water to make the egg wash. Brush the challah with the egg wash, making sure to get the nooks and crannies and all around the sides. Cover with kitchen towel and let it rise in that warm spot for at least an hour until it's double the size.

Preheat the oven to 350°F (175°C). Combine the poppy seeds, sesame seeds, garlic flakes, onion flakes and salt in a small bowl. Brush the challah with the egg wash again and sprinkle the topping all over the challah. Bake for 30–35 minutes until golden. Rotate the pan once through the baking for even browning. When you tap on the bread it should sound fairly hollow.

Let cool completely before breaking into the challah . . . which is impossible. Good luck.

HARISSA LAMB MEATBALLS

"SPIIIIICCCCY" – STEFON, *SATURDAY NIGHT LIVE*

Bambalamballs. If you don't love spice, take down the amount of hot paprika and harissa. But come on . . . grow a pair! If you're using store-bought harissa, taste it before you add it to the sauce to check its spice level. Keep in mind that this sauce's heat intensifies as it cooks. Spice with caution.

MAKES 4 SERVINGS

INGREDIENTS

LAMB BALLS

5 cloves garlic, minced

¾ cup (36 g) cilantro, chopped finely

½ cup (24 g) parsley, chopped finely

1 lb (454 g) ground lamb

⅓ cup (36 g) plain breadcrumbs

1 large egg

1 ½ tbsp (23 ml) olive oil

1 tsp salt

½ tsp turmeric

¼ tsp fresh black pepper

¼ tsp cumin

Pinch of cinnamon

HARISSA SAUCE

2 tbsp (30 ml) olive oil

7 cloves garlic, minced

1 ¼ cups (30 g) cilantro, chopped finely

½ cup (12 g) parsley, chopped finely

1 ½ tbsp (10 g) paprika

1 ½ tsp (3 g) turmeric

1 ½ tsp (3 g) hot paprika

26 ½ oz (780 ml) strained tomato sauce

1 tbsp (13 g) tomato paste

2-4 tbsp (26-52 g) Ancho Chili Harissa
(page 215), or store bought

2 tbsp (30 ml) water

1 tsp salt

1 long hot red pepper

Chopped cilantro

METHOD

In a large bowl, gently combine the ingredients for the lamb balls. Set aside.

To prepare the harissa sauce, heat the olive oil in a large sauté pan with a tight-fitting lid over medium heat. Add the garlic, cilantro, parsley, paprika, turmeric and hot paprika. Sauté while stirring for about a minute to release the flavors and aromas. Stir in the tomato sauce, tomato paste, harissa, water and salt.

While the sauce is coming to a simmer, form the lamb mixture into 32–35 small balls and drop them gently into the sauce in one layer, making sure they are not sitting on top of each other. Add the hot pepper into the sauce.

Once the sauce is at a gentle simmer, turn the heat down to low and cover the pan. Cook and *swirl* the pan occasionally. Do not try to mix the meatballs and sauce with a wooden spoon or other tool or you may "hurt" them. Swirl the pan when you get the urge, it will keep the meatballs from falling apart. Cook for 25 minutes or until the lamb balls are cooked through and the sauce is fragrant and thick.

Garnish with chopped cilantro.

RICOTTA & ZA'ATAR RAVIOLI

WITH WHOLE EGG YOLKS

This is not your typical Friday-night appetizer. It's luxurious and decadent, and Friday is the time for it. This recipe calls for almost a whole carton of eggs. #ballin. It's very impressive, so save it for a time your in-laws are coming over for dinner. At first glance, they look like your basic ravioli. Once broken into, the beautiful yolk starts pouring onto the plate and creates the sauce for the dish. The ricotta and za'atar flavor combination here works nicely, giving the dish even more creaminess. Italians would approve.

MAKES 4–8 SERVINGS (8 LARGE RAVIOLI)

INGREDIENTS

PASTA DOUGH
1 cup (125 g) all-purpose flour
½ tsp salt
1 large egg
2 egg yolks
½ tbsp (8 ml) olive oil

FILLING
1 cup (250 g) ricotta
¼ cup (28 g) grated Parmesan cheese
1 tbsp (9 g) za'atar
½ tsp salt

8 egg yolks, fresh and organic
7 tbsp (100 g) unsalted butter
Lemon zest
Grated Parmesan
Chopped chives

METHOD

To make the pasta dough, place the flour and salt in a food processor and pulse until combined and the flour is finer. Add the egg, yolks and olive oil and pulse until the dough forms a ball of sorts. This will take about a minute until it comes together. If the dough is too dry and won't come together, add a teaspoon more of olive oil and pulse again. Remove the dough from the processor and lightly knead it into a tight ball. Cover with two layers of plastic wrap and let it rest for 40 minutes. When you poke the dough, it should not spring back.

To make the filling, combine the ricotta, Parmesan, za'atar and salt.

Cut the dough into 4 equal portions. Working in batches, roll the dough in a pasta machine dusted with flour. When you're not working with any pasta dough, rolled or not, keep it covered with a kitchen towel to prevent it from drying out. Roll the dough thin enough that you can see your hand through it.

Lay the pasta sheet on a lightly floured surface. Brush the whole pasta sheet very lightly with water. Dollop 2 tablespoons (35 g) of filling onto the pasta sheet, evenly spaced out leaving at least 3 inches (7.5 cm) of space between them. Using the back of a spoon, create a well in the center of the filling. Gently lay the egg yolks in the center of the well taking care not to break them. Season the yolks with salt and fresh black pepper. Cover the filling and yolk with a second sheet of pasta dough. Seal the filling inside with your fingers, making sure that no air is trapped in the ravioli.

Cut the ravioli into 4-inch (10-cm) squares and transfer them to a flour-dusted baking sheet. Keep them covered with a kitchen towel until they're ready to be boiled. Continue making the ravioli with the remaining dough.

Bring a large pot of salted water to a boil and begin melting the butter in a large sauté pan over medium heat. Boil the ravioli for 2 ½ minutes. As soon as the pasta is cooked through, transfer the ravioli, gently, to the pan with a slotted spoon. Make sure that the side of the ravioli with the egg yolk is facing up in the pan. This will ensure that the yolk won't cook any further. Sauté in the melted butter for 1–2 minutes.

Season with salt, lemon zest and grated Parmesan cheese. Remove the ravioli from the pan onto the serving dish. Garnish the ravioli with chopped chives and serve.

FISH KTZIZOT

IN AGRISTADA

Normally used with chicken or meat, *agristada* is a lemon egg-based sauce. Jews who follow the rules of kashrut will use an *agristada* sauce in place of a cream-based sauce since it's not kosher to mix meat and dairy. I was trying to find a good sauce to go with these fish cakes that wasn't a tomato-based sauce. This was my mom's genius idea. "It's like a piccata sauce!" Mom always knows best. Oh, *ktzizot* is just the Hebrew word for balls . . . meatballs.

MAKES 4 SERVINGS

INGREDIENTS

KTZITZOT

½ yellow onion

⅓ cup (8 g) chopped cilantro

1 lb (454 g) fresh tilapia

½ tsp salt

¼ tsp cumin

1 large egg

1 tbsp (6 g) plain bread crumbs

1 ½ cups (160 g) plain bread crumbs

Salt and fresh black pepper

Canola oil for frying

AGRISTADA

2 eggs

2 tbsp (30 ml) olive oil

1 tbsp (8 g) all-purpose flour

1 ½ cups (360 ml) water

¼ cup (60 ml) lemon juice

Salt and fresh black pepper

2 tbsp (20 g) capers

Chopped parsley

Thin lemon slices

METHOD

To make the ktzitzot, pulse the onion and cilantro in a food processor until finely chopped. Cut the tilapia into smaller pieces to fit nicely in the food processor. Add the fish and pulse until the fish is finely chopped but not pasty. When you press it together with your fingers, it should hold together.

Transfer the fish mixture to a large bowl and add the salt, cumin, egg and bread crumbs. Mix gently using your hands until combined evenly.

Shape the ktzitzot into flat patties. You should end up with 8–10 ktzitzot. Place the bread crumbs in a shallow bowl and season with salt and fresh black pepper.

Heat ¼ inch (6 mm) of oil in a fry pan over medium-low heat. Bread each side of the patties and place them straight into the oil. Fry for 2–2 ½ minutes on each side until golden brown and cooked though. Drain them on a paper-towel-lined baking sheet. Season with salt when they come out of the oil. Do this in batches and don't crowd the ktzitzot in the pan.

To make the sauce, whisk the eggs, olive oil and flour together until homogenous in a large bowl. Heat the water and lemon juice in saucepan over medium-high heat until it comes to a simmer. Let cool for 2 minutes. Slowly stream the hot mixture into the bowl with the egg mixture while whisking vigorously to temper the eggs. Don't do this too quickly or the eggs will scramble.

Once you've whisked in all of the water and lemon mixture, transfer the sauce to a back into the pan and heat over medium-low heat, stirring constantly until thickened and warmed through. Season with salt and fresh black pepper and stir in the capers.

Plate each serving dish with a bit of sauce. Place the fish ktzizot on top of the sauce and spoon a bit more over each one. Garnish with chopped parsley and lemon slices.

LEMON CHICKEN WITH OLIVES

ZINGALICIOUS! THAT'S A WORD.

I've got both my parents making this recipe for their friends. That is how I know I've succeeded. This chicken is tangy and packed with so much flavor. It looks vibrant and tastes just as bright. Normally this is made in a tajine—a clay dish that acts as its own oven. I know most people don't own one, so I've substituted a pot for this traditional Moroccan way of preparing chicken (it's still just as delicious). I've also improved on the cooking method. I build the flavors gradually instead of throwing it all in and turning the heat on. It gives the dish more character and depth. You can use either preserved or fresh lemons as long as you adjust for salt content as you cook, as you should *always* do, anyway.

MAKES 4 SERVINGS

INGREDIENTS

8 pieces skin-on, bone-in chicken drumsticks and/or thighs

Salt and fresh black pepper to taste

1 tbsp (15 ml) olive oil

1 large yellow onion, cut into ¼-inch (6-mm) slices

2 cloves garlic, minced

½ tbsp (9 g) grated fresh ginger

1 tbsp (7 g) paprika

2 tsp (5 g) cumin

1 tsp turmeric

½ cup (120 ml) white wine

2 cups (480 ml) chicken broth (homemade is always better)

1 Preserved Lemon (page 223), rinsed, cut into 8 wedges

1 cup (160 g) pitted green Spanish olives

2 tbsp (30 ml) fresh lemon juice

Chopped cilantro

METHOD

Preheat the oven to 325°F (165°C). Season the chicken well with salt and fresh black pepper on both sides. Heat the olive oil in a large Dutch oven or ovenproof pot over medium-high heat. Sear the chicken on each side until golden brown, about 4–5 minutes per side. Don't try to lift the chicken if it is stuck to the bottom of the pot! That means it's not ready to be flipped. It will release once it has browned properly. Do this in batches if needed.

Remove the chicken from the pot and add the onion. Stir and cook for 6–7 minutes until the onion has softened and picked up a bit of color. Stir in the garlic, ginger, paprika, cumin and turmeric. Sauté for 30 seconds just to release the aromas. Deglaze with white wine and be sure to scrape the bottom of the pot to release the flavor bits. Add the chicken back in and pour the chicken broth over top.

Turn the heat up to high and bring the broth to a boil. As soon as it begins to boil, turn the heat off and add the preserved lemon wedges and olives. Cover and braise in the oven for 50 minutes until the chicken is incredibly tender and cooked through.

Remove the chicken from the pot and bring the sauce up to a boil. Reduce by half until it has thickened, about 5–6 minutes. Stir in the fresh lemon juice and taste for seasoning. Add salt if needed. Turn the heat off and return the chicken to the sauce delicately.

Garnish with chopped cilantro before serving.

MEATBALLS IN WHITE WINE & PEA SAUCE

WITH JERUSALEM ARTICHOKE MASH

This is a spin on the classic meatballs and mash. I've mixed the meat with a combination of spices used in Middle Eastern cooking that enhances the flavor of beef and lamb. The Jerusalem artichokes, or sunchokes, have a distinct flavor that goes really well with the meatballs. Also, these meatballs are massive . . . like, softball size.

MAKES 4 SERVINGS

INGREDIENTS

MEATBALLS

⅔ lb (300 g) ground beef chuck
½ lb (225 g) ground lamb
3 cloves garlic, minced
½ cup (45 g) plain bread crumbs
1 large egg
2 ½ tbsp (4 g) chopped dill
1 ½ tbsp (2 g) chopped parsley
1 tbsp (1.5 g) chopped mint
1 ½ tsp (4 g) cumin
1 tsp salt
½ tsp coriander
½ tsp cinnamon
Pinch cloves
Pinch allspice
Pinch nutmeg

SUNCHOKE MASH

10 large sunchokes
1 medium white potato
3 tbsp (42 g) unsalted butter
¼ cup (60 ml) heavy cream (35%–40%)
½ tsp salt

1 ½ tbsp (23 ml) olive oil

WHITE WINE SAUCE

1 tbsp (14 g) unsalted butter
6 cloves garlic, minced
1 tbsp (8 g) all-purpose flour
1 ½ cups (360 ml) dry white wine
1 cup (240 ml) chicken stock
½ cup (75 g) frozen or fresh peas
¼ cup (6 g) chopped dill
¼ tsp salt
¼ tsp fresh black pepper

METHOD

In a large bowl, combine all the ingredients for the meatballs using your hands. Try not to overmix this. Cover with plastic wrap and set in the fridge for at least one hour to marry the flavors. This can be done up to 24 hours ahead.

While the meat is resting, make the sunchoke mash. Bring a pot of salted water to a boil. Peel the sunchokes and potato. Cut into 1-inch (2.5-cm) cubes and immediately drop them into the boiling water to prevent browning. Cook until fork-tender, 10–12 minutes. Drain well and return them to the pot. Add the butter, heavy cream and salt. Using a potato masher or wire whisk, mash the sunchokes and potatoes while mixing with the butter and cream. Mash until you reach your desired consistency. I prefer the mash to be a bit chunky. Cover and set aside.

Preheat the oven to 400°F (205°C). Form the meat mixture into 4 large meatballs. Heat the olive oil in a large ovenproof skillet over medium heat. Season the meatballs with salt and pepper. Sear the meatballs on all sides until nicely browned, about 3 minutes per side. Transfer the skillet to the oven and roast until the meatballs are cooked through, about 12 minutes or until a meat thermometer reads 155°F (68°C) on the inside of one of the meatballs.

Remove the skillet from the oven and gently transfer the meatballs to a plate. Cover it with tinfoil and let them rest.

To make the white wine sauce, heat the butter in that same skillet over medium heat. Add the garlic and sauté for 30 seconds until fragrant. Stir in the flour and cook for another 30 seconds. Deglaze the pan with the white wine, making sure to scrape the bottom of the skillet to release any flavor bits. Turn the heat up to high and bring to a boil. Stir in the chicken stock and reduce the sauce until it has thickened. Stir in the peas and cook for 1–2 minutes. Turn the heat off and stir in the dill, salt and pepper.

Plate the sunchoke mash onto each serving plate. Top the mash with a meatball and spoon the sauce over the top.

SIMMERED RED SNAPPER

WITH FINGERLINGS AND CHICKPEAS

When one thinks of Moroccan cooking, fish in a red sauce is what usually comes to mind. This is one of those classic Moroccan fish dishes. More often than not, when I'm on the phone with one of my parents asking them what I should make for dinner, they describe a version of this fish: "It's so simple. Take a large pan, line it with tomato slices. . . ." Each time it's slightly different, but the method is always the same. I've made this version a bit more fancy—posh, if you will—than the Moroccan fish I've seen come out of my family's kitchens. It's absolutely beautiful, isn't it?

MAKES 4 SERVINGS

INGREDIENTS

⅛ tsp saffron

¼ cup (60 ml) water, just boiled

1 tbsp (15 ml) olive oil

3 Roma tomatoes, cut into ⅓-inch (8-mm) slices

4 cloves garlic, crushed and roughly chopped

2 small carrots, peeled and cut into 3-inch (7.5-cm) sticks

6 fingerling potatoes, cut in half lengthwise

1 cup (165 g) canned chickpeas, drained and rinsed

2 long hot green peppers

¼ cup (6 g) chopped cilantro

1 ½ tbsp (10 g) paprika

2 tsp (4 g) turmeric

¼ tsp cumin

¼ tsp cardamom

1 tsp salt

Fresh black pepper

3 cups (720 ml) water

2 deboned skin-on red snapper fillets

4 slices lemon

4 cups (692 g) cooked couscous to serve

Chopped cilantro

METHOD

Place the saffron in a small bowl and add the just-boiled water. Set aside to steep.

In a large, deep pan with fitted lid, heat the olive oil over medium-low heat. Lay the slices of tomato along the bottom of the pan. Top with the garlic, carrots, potatoes, chickpeas, long peppers and cilantro. Season with the paprika, turmeric, cumin, cardamom, salt and pepper to taste. Top with 3 cups (720 ml) of water. Everything should basically be submerged.

Turn the heat up to high and bring to a boil. Turn down to a simmer and cover the pan. Simmer for 15 minutes to soften and cook the vegetables and chickpeas.

With a sharp knife, slash the skin side of the snapper. Make sure not to slice the whole way through! This is simply to allow more flavor to enter the fish. Season the snapper with salt on both sides. Lay the fillets skin side up on top of the vegetables in the pan. They will not be fully submerged. Place the lemon slices on top of the fish. Partially cover the pan and continue simmering for 12–14 minutes basting the fish with the cooking liquid every few minutes. The fish should be *just* done and flaky.

Place a cup (173 g) of couscous into each serving dish. Top with a piece of fish, vegetables and lots of cooking liquid. Garnish with chopped cilantro.

CHICKEN LIVER OVER CREAMY CORN POLENTA

WITH CARAMELIZED ONIONS. DON'T BE SHY.

Chicken liver is one of those things that you have to grow up on to love. I did, and I *love* it. The best way to take it down is to pan-fry it with a ton of oil and eat it right out of the pan with a baguette. You see a decent amount of chicken liver in Israeli cooking, normally stuffed in a pita with other innards after being grilled. Stop cringing. It's scrumptious. I used yellow corn grits instead of the fine-ground polenta. I like the final texture a lot better. Please use corn grits!

MAKES 4 SERVINGS

INGREDIENTS

CARAMELIZED ONIONS

1 ½ tbsp (23 ml) olive oil

½ tbsp (7 g) unsalted butter

1 ½ large onions, sliced ¼-inch (6-mm) thick

¼ tsp salt

POLENTA

4 ⅓ cups (1 liter) chicken stock

1 ¼ cups (160 g) yellow corn grits

1 tsp salt

2 cobs of white or yellow corn, kernels cut off

1 ½ cups (360 ml) heavy cream (35%–40%)

5 tbsp (70 g) unsalted butter

LIVERS

1 lb (454 g) chicken livers

Salt and fresh black pepper

2 ½ tbsp (38 ml) olive oil

2 tbsp (28 g) unsalted butter

1 tbsp (1.5 g) chopped thyme

White balsamic vinegar

Chopped cornichons or gherkins

Chopped parsley

Maldon salt

METHOD

For the caramelized onions, heat the olive oil and butter over low heat in a large sauté pan with lid. Add the sliced onions, sprinkle with the salt and cover. Cook, covered, for about 25 minutes, stirring every so often. Remove the lid, turn the heat up to medium and continue cooking, stirring often for another 10–15 minutes. The onions will become a deep caramel color. They may need an additional 5–10 minutes to get to their deepest color. This takes time. Do not rush it! Turn the heat off when you've achieved the desired caramelization.

While the onions are caramelizing, make the polenta by bringing the chicken stock to a boil in a pot with fitted lid. Once it comes to a boil, whisk in the corn grits and salt. Immediately turn the heat down to low. Stir in the corn kernels. Cook, stirring frequently for 12–15 minutes until thick and almost dry looking. Turn the heat off and stir in the heavy cream and butter.

Before frying the livers, clean and trim away any fat or connective tissue. Pat them dry with a paper towel to remove as much moisture as possible. Season them generously with salt and lots of black pepper. Remove the onions from the sauté pan. Heat the olive oil, butter and thyme over medium-high heat. Add the livers and fry for 3 minutes per side. Be careful: The oil will jump. Use a splatter screen over the pan as the livers fry. Once the livers are cooked, return the onions to the pan and toss.

Plate the polenta onto each serving dish, top with the livers and onions and drizzle a bit of white balsamic vinegar over the top for some brightness. Scatter some sliced cornichons over the dish, garnish with chopped parsley and season with some Maldon salt.

KEBAB & SHRIMP PAELLA

AN ISRAELI & A SPANIARD MAKE LOVE...

I've always been in love with paella. But after my three-year anniversary/honeymoon trip to Spain, it's become a bit of an obsession. I carried back two paella pans to the States by hand so they wouldn't warp on me. This dish just felt right. It happened so naturally that I'm surprised it's a fairly new concept: Middle Eastern paella. You can use any type of sausage you like. I happen to really enjoy beef wieners. Chicken sausages would be delightful here too. Don't be afraid to give that rice on the bottom a really good char. Color is flavor!

MAKES 4–6 SERVINGS

INGREDIENTS

KOFTA KEBABS

1 large onion

1 ½ lb (680 g) ground beef chuck

¼ lb (113 g) ground lamb

2 tbsp (3 g) chopped cilantro

1 tbsp (1.5 g) chopped parsley

1 tbsp (15 ml) olive oil

1 ¼ tsp (7 g) salt

½ tsp cumin

½ tsp paprika

¼ tsp fresh black pepper

¼ tsp baking powder

Pinch allspice

6 strands saffron

¼ cup (60 ml) olive oil

1 large yellow onion, diced

1 ½ tsp (3 g) turmeric

1 tsp salt

¼ tsp cumin

Fresh black pepper

2 smoked beef sausages, sliced into 8 pieces on the bias

¾ cup (155 g) Bomba rice or short-grain rice, rinsed

8–10 pieces shell-on shrimp, deveined

½ cup (85 g) shelled fresh or frozen fava beans

2 tbsp (30 ml) fresh lemon juice

Chopped cilantro

METHOD

To make the kebabs, grate the onion in a food processor with grater attachment or by hand on the large-hole side of a box grater. In a large bowl, mix the grated onion, beef, lamb, cilantro, parsley, olive oil, salt, cumin, paprika, pepper, baking powder and allspice until just combined. Shape the kebabs into 4-inch (10-cm) long torpedo shapes. You should get about 8 of them.

Steep the saffron by placing it in a small bowl with ¼ cup (60 ml) just-boiled water. Set aside.

Heat the oil over medium-low heat in a 10–12-inch (25–30-cm) paella pan. You can also use a cast-iron skillet or just a large frying pan. Add the onions and sauté until translucent, about 4 minutes. Stir in the turmeric, salt, cumin and black pepper to taste. Sauté for another minute to release the flavor and aroma of the spices.

Add the kebabs and sausages to the pan. Cook for 2–3 minutes per side until lightly browned. Arrange the kebabs and sausages around the outside of the paella pan. Add the rice into the pan in the middle and around the meats. Try to make sure you're not getting any grains on top of the kebabs or sausages. Immediately pour boiling water over the rice in the middle of the pan until it comes about halfway up the kebabs. Add the saffron and the water it had been steeping in.

Let this simmer for 25–30 minutes, adding water as needed until the rice is cooked through. This is kind of like making risotto, just without the stirring. Don't attempt to stir this at all.

Once the rice is cooked through, turn the heat up to medium-high and arrange the shrimp in the middle on top of the rice. Scatter the fava beans around the pan and cover with a sheet pan for 2–3 minutes until the shrimp is cooked through. Remove the "lid" and listen to the rice in the pan. It should sound like it's drier and getting crispy. Let this cook for another 2 minutes until the rice has formed a nice crust along the bottom.

Pour the lemon juice all around the pan for a burst of freshness and acidity. Garnish with *a lot* of chopped cilantro. Like, at least 3 tablespoons (45 g)!

MOROCCAN SPICED SHEPHERD'S PIE

WHEN WORLDS COLLIDE

I don't think anyone in Israel knows what shepherd's pie is. There is, however, a similar dish called *siniyet batata*, which literally translates to "tray of potatoes." If the two dishes made love, you'd get this bouncing baby recipe. That sounds weird. . . . The combination of the *baharat* seasoning with the beef gives the dish its distinctive Moroccan flavor. I've swapped out the mashed-potato crust for sliced potatoes, which soak up all the delicious fat that releases from the ground meat. I love adding pine nuts to give a nice nutty flavor depth, too. It's just so good!

MAKES 6 SERVINGS

INGREDIENTS

1 tbsp (15 ml) olive oil

1 large yellow onion, finely diced

4 small carrots, cut into ½-inch (13-mm) pieces

1 ½ lb (680 g) ground beef chuck

2 tbsp (36 g) grated fresh ginger

1 tbsp (7 g) paprika

1 ½ tsp (4 g) cumin

1 tsp cinnamon

½ tsp coriander

¼ tsp nutmeg

1 ½ tsp (9 g) salt

Freshly ground black pepper

1 ½ tbsp (20 g) tomato paste

2 tbsp (16 g) all-purpose flour

¼ cup (35 g) pine nuts

⅓ cup (16 g) chopped parsley

2 cups (480 ml) beef stock

5 white potatoes, peeled

⅓ cup (50 g) frozen or fresh peas

1 tbsp (15 ml) olive oil

Paprika

Salt and fresh black pepper

Chopped parsley

METHOD

Heat the olive oil in a large sauté pan with a fitted lid over medium heat. Add the chopped onion and carrots to the pan and sauté until they begin to soften, about 5–7 minutes. Add the ground beef. Using a wooden spoon, break up the beef as it cooks. Once it is no longer pink, add the ginger, paprika, cumin, cinnamon, coriander, nutmeg, salt, pepper and tomato paste. Continue cooking for 5 minutes. Add the flour and sauté for another 2 minutes to cook out the floury flavor. Add the pine nuts, parsley and beef stock to the pan. Bring the filling up to a low boil. Turn the heat down to low, cover the pan and simmer for 20 minutes.

Preheat oven to 400°F (205°C).

Put the peeled potatoes in a pot and cover them with cold water. Place the pot over high heat. Once the water comes to a boil, cook the potatoes for 12–15 minutes. They should be undercooked and slightly firm. Drain the potatoes and cool on a cutting board. Slice into ½-inch (12-mm) slices.

Stir the peas into the beef filling and transfer it into an 8-inch-by-11-inch (20-cm-x-28-cm) baking dish. Arrange the potatoes on top of the filling, making sure to overlap them. Brush the potatoes with the olive oil and season generously with paprika, salt and pepper.

Bake for an hour until the filling is bubbly and the potatoes are golden brown and cooked through. Let rest for at least 10 minutes before serving. Garnish with chopped parsley.

"SMOKED" & ROASTED WHOLE CAULIFLOWER

TOPPED WITH GARLIC PANKO AND TAHINI

I'm treating this whole cauliflower like a nice piece of meat—boiling it in a smoky, pickley brine and then roasting it in a hot oven. I wish you could taste it through the pages of this book. It's soft on the inside and crispy on the outside. No need for an outdoor smoker since I used liquid smoke, creating a deep, full flavor. If I had it my way, I would batter the whole thing and fry it, but my love handles don't need that.

MAKES 2 SERVINGS, OR 4 SERVINGS AS A SIDE

INGREDIENTS

1 large whole cauliflower
3 qt (2.8 L) water
¼ cup plus 1 tbsp (75 ml) liquid smoke
2 tbsp (8 g) pickling spice
1 tbsp (20 g) coarse kosher salt
2 tsp (10 ml) honey
Olive oil
Salt

GARLIC PANKO

½ cup (30 g) panko
1 ½ tbsp (21 g) unsalted butter
1 tbsp (15 ml) olive oil
1 clove garlic, sliced thinly
½ cup (45 g) panko
Salt and fresh black pepper

1 tbsp (9 g) pine nuts
Tahini (page 212)
Schug (page 220), optional
Lemon zest

METHOD

Preheat the oven to 475°F (245°C). Remove the leaves from the stem of the cauliflower. Cut the stem so that the cauliflower sits upright on its own.

Bring the water, liquid smoke, pickling spice, salt and honey to a boil in a 6 quart (5.7 L) stockpot. Turn the heat down to low and gently lower the cauliflower into the brine. It's okay if it is not fully submerged. Simmer the cauliflower, turning it halfway through cooking, for 14 minutes. Carefully remove the cauliflower from the brine and place it in a greased roasting pan or ovenproof skillet. Drizzle the cauliflower with a good amount of olive oil and season with salt. Roast it in the oven for 40–45 minutes until nicely browned all over.

To make the garlic panko, heat the butter, olive oil and sliced garlic in a sauté pan over medium-low heat. Once the garlic is fragrant, about 30 seconds, add in the panko. Cook and toss for 3–4 minutes until they're toasty and golden brown. Season with salt and pepper to taste and remove them from the pan. Set aside.

Toast the pine nuts in a dry pan over medium heat while tossing for 1–2 minutes.

When the cauliflower is ready, place it on the serving dish and pour a decent amount of tahini over it, top with garlic panko, pine nuts, dollop a few spoonfuls of schug (optional) and garnish with lemon zest.

BEACH

JUST LIKE SITTING
IN THE SAND IN TEL AVIV

Without fail, everyone in Tel Aviv arrives at the beach at some point on a Saturday, either to tan, play a friendly game of *matkot*, have a beer, hang with family, power-walk along the water or to grab a bite with friends. This happens year-round if weather allows, and it normally does. The beaches are lined with restaurants that deliver food straight to your chair in the water. You don't have to move unless you want to. I don't. I am what an Israeli would call a "stomach/back"—shifting only when the sun does. Hmm . . . some things just don't translate well from Hebrew to English. This is a collection of dishes that you would find at a beach restaurant in Tel Aviv with a modern twist. These recipes are great for barbecues too! They're full of seafood, veggies and freshness. My personal favorite is the Peel & Eat Harissa Shrimp (page 65). Oof. So spicy and so good. Then wash it down with a super-fresh Limonana (page 82). That just screams beach.

FATTOUSH

QUINTESSENTIAL

Fifty percent of this salad is packed with fresh vegetables and the other fifty percent is generally deep-fried pita. I wish you could see the elation on my face. Genius. I like to call it the Middle Eastern *panzanella*. Thanks to whoever was the first to make it. This is the salad that will make you fall in love with sumac. It adds a lemony flavor to anything. There is no substitute. To keep things light for this salad (and my waistline), the pita is baked until golden brown and crispy instead of deep-fried.

MAKES 1–2 SERVINGS, OR 4 SERVINGS AS A SIDE

INGREDIENTS

1 day-old pita, torn into 1-inch (2.5-cm) pieces

1 ½ tbsp (23 ml) olive oil

Maldon salt

1 Roma tomato, diced

1 kirby cucumber, sliced or diced

2 radishes, cut in ⅛-inch (3-mm)-thick slices or thinner

⅛ cup (13 g) sliced red onions, paper thin

1 scallion, sliced on diagonal

¼ cup (7 g) arugula or rocket

1 tsp sumac

1 ½ tbsp (23 ml) lemon juice

2 tsp (10 ml) olive oil

Maldon salt

¼ cup (28 g) crumbled Bulgarian feta cheese

METHOD

Preheat the oven to 375°F (190°C).

Toss the torn pita, olive oil and Maldon salt to taste in a bowl. Transfer the pita to a tinfoil-lined baking sheet for easy cleanup. Toast in the oven for 8–10 minutes until golden brown and crisp.

In a large bowl, toss the pita chips, tomato, cucumber, radishes, red onion, scallion, arugula, sumac, lemon juice, olive oil and Maldon salt to taste until evenly coated. Do this using your hands so you do not "injure" the delicate vegetables.

If you would like to arrange the radishes as I did in the photo, toss them separately.

Arrange the salad on the serving dish and crumble the feta over top. Season with some more sumac and Maldon salt if desired.

PEEL & EAT HARISSA SHRIMP

GET YOUR HANDS DIRTY

Shrimp is not kosher. But that's not to say that almost every seafood restaurant in Tel Aviv doesn't serve it. I used to get a plate of grilled shrimp, or "shreemps" as my cousin would say, every time I was at the beach. My version is peel and eat with spicy harissa. The shrimp are cooked in their shells for flavor and get coated in hot harissa and lemon. When you peel the shrimp with your hands, just enough of the flavor and heat get transferred onto that shrimp. It's actually perfect.

4 SERVINGS

INGREDIENTS

1 lb (454 g) shell-on headless shrimp

1–3 tbsp (13–40 g) Ancho Chili Harissa (page 215) or store bought

1 tbsp (15 ml) olive oil

½ tsp salt

1 ½ tbsp (23 ml) olive oil

1 lemon, cut in half

Chopped parsley

METHOD

To devein the shell-on shrimp, cut down the back of each one with scissors and pull out the vein.

In a large bowl, toss the deveined shrimp, harissa, olive oil and salt. Cover and refrigerate for 1 hour.

Heat the olive oil in a large skillet on high heat. Sear the shrimp in one layer, making sure there is no overlap, for 2–3 minutes on each side. Just before the shrimp is ready, place the lemon halves in the skillet cut-side-down to pick up some color and flavor.

Alternatively, you can throw the marinated shrimp on a preheated grill, indoor or outdoor.

Before eating, squeeze the lemon over the shrimp and garnish with chopped parsley. Bring napkins.

BUCKWHEAT AND EGGPLANT SALAD

WITH CREAMY LABANE

You'll find eggplant in all dishes in Israel—from time-consuming stews and sauces to salads, like this recipe. This dish is easy to make ahead of time and tastes great cold or at room temperature, which is why it would be enjoyable on a hot day at the beach. Buckwheat has an intense earthy flavor and is balanced out with the labane in this dish. Either way, the grain's still pretty intense, so if you feel like you would be turned off from making this salad because of it, feel free to swap it for farro or even brown rice.

MAKES 4 SERVINGS

INGREDIENTS

1 eggplant, cut into 1-inch (2.5-cm) cubes

⅓ cup (80 ml) olive oil

½ tsp salt

Fresh black pepper

½ cup (85 g) buckwheat groats

3 tbsp (45 ml) lemon juice

1 tbsp (15 ml) olive oil

Salt to taste

2 tbsp (3 g) chopped mint

1 cup (250 g) Labane (page 219), or store bought

Olive oil

Lemon zest

Maldon salt

METHOD

Preheat the oven to 400°F (205°C).

Toss the eggplant with the olive oil, salt and fresh pepper. Spread the eggplant out on a greased baking sheet and roast in the oven for 25–30 minutes, turning the eggplant halfway through roasting.

Cook the buckwheat in a large pot of salted boiling water for 10–12 minutes. Drain and immediately toss with the lemon juice, olive oil and salt while still warm.

Combine the buckwheat, eggplant and chopped mint in a large bowl and taste for seasoning.

Spread the labane on the bottom of each serving dish and top with the buckwheat and eggplant mixture. Drizzle with a good amount of olive oil. Garnish with lemon zest and Maldon salt.

SPICED BEEF MINI BURGERS

WITH DILL YOGURT SAUCE AND SUMAC ONION SALAD

I call these mini burgers because they are smaller than your average burger but not slider-small. This recipe makes 8 minis, which you can easily change to make 4 normal-size burgers. I just like the ratio of beef to bun with mini burgers. The yogurt sauce with dill is the perfect accompaniment to the spices in the meat. I top mine so high with sumac onions that my husband can smell me coming after having one. If you're like me, double the onion recipe.

MAKES 4 SERVINGS (8 MINI BURGERS)

INGREDIENTS

BURGER MEAT

1 ½ lbs (680 g) ground beef chuck

4 cloves garlic, minced

½ cup (12 g) chopped cilantro

3 tbsp (12 g) plain bread crumbs

1 tsp salt

½ tsp cumin

¼ tsp coriander

YOGURT SAUCE

1 cup (250 g) Greek yogurt

3 tbsp (5 g) chopped dill

1 ½ tbsp (23 ml) lemon juice

2 cloves garlic, minced

1 tbsp (15 ml) water

SUMAC ONIONS

1 cup (160 g) thinly sliced red onions

1 tbsp (6 g) sumac

2 tsp (10 ml) lemon juice

Salt to taste

Salt and fresh black pepper to season

8 brioche mini buns or dinner rolls

METHOD

Combine the ingredients for the burgers, cover and set in the fridge for 30 minutes or overnight.

To make the yogurt sauce, combine the yogurt, dill, lemon juice, garlic and water. Cover and set it in the fridge until you're ready to assemble the burgers.

To make the sumac onion, combine the red onion, sumac, lemon juice and salt to taste. Cover and set it in the fridge until you're ready to assemble.

Form the meat mixture into 8 equal balls and then flatten them to make the patties. You can also make 4 larger burgers. Heat a griddle or frying pan over medium heat. Season both sides of the patties very well. Sear the burgers for 3-4 minutes per side until they form a nice crust on the outside. Do this in batches so you don't crowd the pan. Remove the burgers from the pan and immediately place the cut side of both the top and bottom halves of the buns into the grease. Toast for 1 minute until slightly golden brown.

Assemble the burgers with yogurt sauce on both top and bottom halves of the buns, one patty and a generous amount of sumac onions.

SALMON CEVICHE

WITH AVOCADO, FENNEL SALAD AND ZA'ATAR PITA CHIPS

Seafood is abundant in Israel. This is a simple dish that isn't Middle Eastern in origin, but ceviche is the best way to showcase a fresh piece of fish. You'll find ceviche in almost all posh Tel Aviv restaurants. Please find the best quality sushi-grade salmon in the market. This works really well with other fish like sea bass or striped bass. Go for whatever is freshest!

MAKES 4 SERVINGS

INGREDIENTS

FENNEL SALAD

½ bulb fennel, sliced thinly

1 tsp lemon juice

Salt to taste

White pepper to taste

ZA'ATAR PITA CHIPS

1 pita, torn into 1-inch (2.5-cm) pieces

1 ½ tbsp (23 ml) olive oil

1 ½ tsp (4 g) za'atar

Maldon salt

SALMON CEVICHE

¾ lb (340 g) sushi-grade salmon fillet, cut into ¼-inch (6–7-mm) cubes

1 ripe avocado, cut into ¼-inch (6–7-mm) cubes

1 scallion, sliced on the bias

1 ½ tbsp (23 ml) lemon juice

½ tsp sesame oil

½ tsp olive oil

Salt to taste

Black sesame seeds to garnish

Maldon salt

Za'atar

METHOD

For the fennel salad, toss the fennel, lemon juice, salt and white pepper to taste in a small bowl. Cover and set in the fridge to marinate for 20 minutes.

Preheat the oven to 375°F (190°C). Toss the torn pita, olive oil, za'atar and Maldon salt to taste in a bowl. Transfer the pita to a tinfoil-lined baking sheet for easy cleanup. Toast in the oven for 8–10 minutes until golden brown and crisp. Set aside.

For the salmon ceviche, combine the salmon, avocado, scallion, lemon juice, sesame oil, olive oil and salt to taste in a bowl. Toss using your hands! Marinate in the fridge for 10 minutes but no longer than 15, otherwise the acid "overcooks" the salmon.

Plate the fennel salad at the bottom of the serving dish, top with the ceviche and garnish with black sesame seeds and Maldon salt and sprinkle with za'atar. Serve with the za'atar pita chips on the side.

SUMAC FRIES

WITH SCHUG MAYO AND HARISSA KETCHUP

I can't go a week without having fries. It's become a problem, so I've had to start baking them at home instead of getting ones that are deep fried. These fries . . . so good. And how about dem dips? Honestly, I would even resort to a carrot as the carrier for the *schug* mayo. I use the dips for a lot of other dishes too. So keep them in mind next time you make chicken fingers at home.

MAKES 4 SERVINGS

INGREDIENTS

SCHUG MAYO
⅓ cup (80 g) mayonnaise
1–2 tsp (6–12 g) Schug (page 220)

HARISSA KETCHUP
⅓ cup (80 g) ketchup
½–1 tbsp (6–13 g) Ancho Chili Harissa (page 216)

SUMAC FRIES
2 russet potatoes, cut into ½-inch (12-mm)-thick sticks
¼ cup (60 ml) olive oil
1 tsp coarse kosher salt

1 tbsp (6 g) sumac
½ tsp Maldon salt

METHOD

Mix the mayo and schug together in a small bowl. In a separate bowl, mix the ketchup and harissa. Cover, and set both aside in the fridge.

Preheat the oven to 450°F (230°C).

Toss the potato with the olive oil and salt to coat all the fries. Spread them evenly on 1 or 2 baking sheets. The more room they have, the crispier they will be.

Bake the fries for 30 minutes turning halfway through the bake. If you want them super crispy, turn the broiler on for 3 minutes to give them some extra color.

As soon as the fries come out of the oven, gently toss them in a bowl with the sumac and Maldon salt. Serve immediately with the schug mayo and harissa ketchup.

CHERMOULA FISH TACOS

TACOS IN TEL AVIV. OR JUST AT HOME.

Chermoula is a sauce made of a mixture of herbs, spices, lemon juice and olive oil and used to flavor fish. It's a Moroccan thing, but after making it, I was convinced that it should be in a Mexican dish. It even looks like a salsa of sorts. I make my chermoula chunkier so that it's got more girth. It's also got a decent kick to it. The preserved lemons add a dimension of flavor that can't be achieved in this sauce otherwise. I use sea bass in this recipe, but cod or tilapia would work just as well. And you could even beer-batter and deep-fry the fish. Mmm. . . .

MAKES 4 SERVINGS

INGREDIENTS

CHERMOULA

¼ cup (60 ml) olive oil

¼ cup (6 g) chopped cilantro

2 ½ tbsp (38 ml) lemon juice

1 tbsp (15 g) grated garlic

½ tbsp (9 g) grated ginger

½ tbsp (9 g) finely chopped Preserved Lemon (page 223), or store bought

½ tsp (1 g) paprika

¼ tsp hot paprika

¼ tsp cumin

Pinch of salt

1 lb (454 g) skinless sea bass fillet, deboned

Paprika

Salt

1 tbsp (15 ml) olive oil

Flour tortillas

Sliced avocado

Shredded cabbage

Cilantro leaves

Limes

Ancho Chili Harissa (page 215), or store bought

Sumac

METHOD

To make the chermoula, combine the olive oil, cilantro, lemon juice, garlic, ginger, preserved lemon, paprika, hot paprika, cumin and salt in a small bowl.

Season the sea bass with paprika and salt to taste on both sides of the fillet. Heat the olive oil in a skillet over medium-low heat. Sear the fillet for 4–5 minutes on each side until cooked through and flaky.

Serve with chermoula, tortillas, avocado, cabbage, cilantro, limes, harissa and sumac and allow everyone to make their own tacos.

SPICY POMELO SALAD

WITH KALAMATA OLIVES

This is a small twist on a spicy orange salad that you find all over Israel. I remember eating pomelo growing up—it was a treat when we could find it in the grocery store. I always managed to find the pomelo with the pink insides. The white ones are perfect too, though. It reminds me of summery days. The combination of flavors hits all the taste buds on your tongue: sweet, sour, bitter and salty. It has it all!

MAKES 4 SERVINGS

INGREDIENTS

¼ pomelo

¼ cup (44 g) pitted and torn kalamata olives

1 tbsp (1.5 g) chopped cilantro

½ tsp lemon juice

¼ tsp hot paprika

¼ tsp paprika

Pinch of salt

Olive oil

METHOD

Segment the pomelo and remove the seeds while shredding the segments. Combine the shredded pomelo with the olives, cilantro, lemon juice, hot paprika, paprika, salt and a small drizzle of olive oil. Toss to combine and serve.

SEARED SESAME TUNA OVER ISRAELI SALAD

A LIGHT AND LOW-FAT DISH

The beach I normally go to in Tel Aviv serves a big bowl of Israeli salad. Because vegetables just don't satisfy me as much as I would like them to, I add canned tuna fish and feta cheese to my salad. I know, sounds strange. I've taken the basic idea of my beach salad and refined it so it's more upscale. It's a great light lunch that won't leave you bloated, especially since you may or may not be in a bikini (or Speedo) while eating it.

MAKES 4 SERVINGS

INGREDIENTS

½ head romaine lettuce, chopped finely
4 kirby cucumbers, diced
4 Roma tomatoes, diced
4 scallions, sliced on the bias
⅛ cup (13 g) diced red onion
2 ½ tbsp (38 ml) lemon juice
2 tbsp (30 ml) olive oil
½ tsp salt
2 ½ lb (230 g) sushi-grade tuna steaks
Salt and fresh black pepper to season
3 tbsp (28 g) sesame seeds
1 tbsp (9 g) black sesame seeds
Sesame oil
Maldon salt

METHOD

Combine the lettuce, cucumbers, tomatoes, scallions, red onion, lemon juice, olive oil and salt in a large bowl and toss.

Season the tuna with lots of salt and black pepper on all sides. Combine the sesame seeds and black sesame seeds in a shallow bowl. Press the tuna steaks into the sesame seeds to form a crust on all sides of the tuna.

Heat a nonstick frying pan on high heat. Sear the tuna for 1 minute on each side for rare tuna. Make sure to sear all edges!

Slice the tuna steaks into ½-inch (12-mm)-thick slices with a sharp knife.

Plate the Israeli salad and top with slices of tuna steak. Drizzle with sesame oil and season with Maldon salt.

PEPPERED WATERMELON & FETA

SUMMER. THIS IS SUMMER.

No trip to the beach is complete without getting watermelon and a side of feta cheese. You watch the sun sink into the horizon as your skin burns from the beating it took all day. You take one bite into that cold watermelon and salty feta, and at that moment, life is absolutely perfect. My version offers a bit more flavor depth because of the hot Korean pepper flakes and olive oil. You can substitute hot paprika for the pepper flakes, if you can't find them.

MAKES 4 SERVINGS

INGREDIENTS

½ watermelon, cut into 1-inch (2.5-cm) cubes

1 tbsp (1.5 g) chopped mint

1 tbsp (15 ml) olive oil

¼ tsp Korean red pepper flakes (Gochugaru)

¼ tsp fresh black pepper

¼ cup (28 g) crumbled French-style creamy feta cheese

Maldon salt

METHOD

Combine the watermelon, mint, olive oil, red pepper flakes and pepper by tossing gently. Cover and marinate in the fridge for 20 minutes.

Plate the watermelon on the serving dish, top with the crumbled feta and season with a little Maldon salt.

LIMONANA

AHHHH, REFRESHING

This is literally the most refreshing thing you can drink on the beach. Okay, maybe a beer trumps it. This is literally the *second* most refreshing thing you can drink on the beach. It's also incredibly simple to make. It won't really last the trek from your house to the beach, but if you're having a backyard BBQ or pool party, you'll want to make this. Leave out the rum for the kiddies, though. I prefer to use 10 Cane rum for this recipe.

MAKES 2 SERVINGS

INGREDIENTS

¼ cup (50 g) sugar

¼ cup (60 ml) boiling water

½ cup (12 g) mint leaves

¼ cup (60 ml) fresh lemon juice

1 cup (140 g) crushed ice

½ cup (120 ml) good-quality light rum

Mint leaves

Lemon slices

METHOD

Combine the sugar and boiling water and mix until the sugar has dissolved. Transfer the sugar water to a blender. Add in the mint leaves, lemon juice, ice and rum. Blend until smooth.

Pour into glasses and garnish with mint leaves and lemon slices. Make a million more.

SLOW COOKING
BUT, OH ... IS IT WORTH THE WAIT

The most delicious dishes take time—a whole lot of waiting. This is not to say that they are difficult to make. They just need a bit more time marinating, brining, resting, roasting or braising. Some of the fare is humble, some elaborate and elegant, but all will impress. This is the kind of cooking that is dear to my heart and creative mind. There is nothing much like roasting a leg of lamb for hours, pulling it out of the oven, lifting the lid and getting hit with the aroma of a slowly cooked piece of meat. Then taking a fork to it and realizing that the meat is literally falling off the bone and shredding apart in the best way possible. The house is filled with a feeling of warmth and love instantly.

CHICKEN AND DUMPLINGS AND DUMPLINGS

KIND OF LIKE A SOUTHERN JEW WITH A STRANGE ACCENT

Chicken soup. Each culture has its own. Jews put matzo balls in theirs. The Chinese make wontons. The Italians use tortellini . . . and so on. Why not have it all? This *is* all of it, and it's the most delicious thing you'll ever have. Shut up. Yes, it is better than your mom's.

MAKES 6 SERVINGS, WITH EXTRA RAVS BECAUSE YOU'LL WANT THEM

INGREDIENTS

STOCK

2 tbsp (30 ml) canola oil

4 whole chicken legs (thigh and drumstick)

1 medium-size beef bone

1 large yellow onion, quartered with peel on

1 medium carrot, cut into thirds

1 medium parsnip, cut in half

1 leek, cut in thirds

½ medium turnip, cut into thirds

¼ small celery root, cut in half

¼ cup (6 g) fresh dill

½ cup (12 g) parsley with stem

2 cloves garlic, crushed

½ tsp (3 g) salt

Fresh black pepper

RAVIOLETTI DOUGH AND FILLING

1 cup (125 g) all-purpose flour

½ tsp salt

1 large egg

2 egg yolks

½ tbsp (8 ml) olive oil

2 tbsp (3 g) chopped dill

Salt and fresh black pepper

Flour for dusting

MATZO DUMPLINGS

⅓ cup plus 1 tbsp (55 g) self-rising flour

⅓ cup (25 g) matzo meal

⅓ cup plus 1 tbsp (95 ml) buttermilk

Salt to taste

Dill for garnish

Fresh black pepper

METHOD

Heat the oil in a large stockpot over medium-high heat. When it's hot, sear the chicken for 5 minutes on each side until it's golden brown. Add the remaining stock ingredients into the pot and cover with 8–10 cups (1.9 L–2.4 L) of water until everything is submerged. Bring the stock up to a boil, then turn the heat down, cover and simmer for at least an hour. Turn the heat off and let cool. I usually do this a day before I'm serving the soup so the flavors get a chance to really marry. Remove the chicken legs and place in a bowl and strain the rest of the ingredients out of the stock. Discard the vegetables and bone. Shred the chicken off the bone and cover until ready to use. Discard the chicken bones.

To make the ravioletti dough, place the flour and salt in a food processor and pulse until combined and the flour is finer. Add the egg, yolks and olive oil and pulse until the dough forms a ball of sorts. If the dough is too dry, add a teaspoon more of olive oil and pulse again. Remove the dough from the processor and lightly knead it into a tight ball. Cover with two layers of plastic wrap and let it rest for 40 minutes.

To make the ravioletti, combine the shredded chicken, chopped dill, salt and fresh black pepper to taste. Divide the dough into 4 equal portions. Working in batches, roll the dough in a pasta machine dusted with flour. When you're not working with any pasta dough, rolled or not, keep it covered with a kitchen towel to prevent it from drying out. The dough should be thin enough to see your hand through it. Lay the pasta sheet on a lightly floured surface. Brush the whole pasta sheet very lightly with water and place a spoonful of the filling, leaving 3 inches (7.5 cm) between them. Cover the filling with a second sheet of pasta dough. Seal the filling inside with your fingers. Cut the ravioletti into 3-inch (7.5-cm) squares. Place them on a baking sheet dusted with flour and cover them with a kitchen towel. Continue making the ravioletti with the remaining dough and filling.

Make the matzo dumpling dough by combining the self-rising flour, matzo meal, buttermilk and salt to taste in a bowl. It should look sticky and very wet.

Just before serving, bring the strained stock to a light boil over medium-high heat. Drop a spoonful of the matzo dumpling dough into the boiling soup. The soup will begin to lighten and thicken as they cook. They're ready when they look pillowy and bouncy—3–4 minutes. Turn the heat off and cover with a lid until the ravioletti is ready.

Bring a large pot of salted boiling water to a boil. Cook the ravioletti until the pasta is cooked through, about 4 minutes.

Place 1–2 ravioletti in each serving bowl, top with hot soup and 1–2 matzo dumplings and garnish with dill and lots of fresh black pepper. Serve immediately.

BRAISED POMEGRANATE SHORT RIBS

OVER PEPPERY FARROTTO

This is one of my favorite dishes in this book. I make really, really good braised short ribs. Humble brag. It's not difficult at all. You just need to follow some simple steps to develop a depth of flavor, and the oven does the rest of the work. I use pomegranate molasses in this recipe because it brings a sweetness and tang to the sauce. Cooking the farro like risotto makes it creamy as hell.

MAKES 4 SERVINGS

INGREDIENTS

1 ⅓ cups (220 g) pearled Italian farro

SHORT RIBS

2 tbsp (30 ml) canola oil

3 ½ lb (1.5 kg) good-quality beef short ribs

Salt and pepper

1 yellow onion, quartered

1 large carrot, peeled and roughly chopped

2 stalks celery, roughly chopped

2 tbsp (16 g) all-purpose flour

½ cup (120 ml) dry red wine

4 cups (960 ml) beef stock

¼ cup (60 ml) pomegranate molasses

2 sprigs rosemary

1 whole head garlic, cut in half through cloves

FARROTTO

2 cups (480 ml) beef stock, divided

2 ⅔ cups (640 ml) water, divided

1 ½ tbsp (23 ml) olive oil

¼ yellow onion, diced finely

1 cup (240 ml) soaking liquid from farro

¼ tsp salt

1 tsp fresh black pepper

¼ cup (60 ml) heavy cream (35%–40%)

2 tbsp (28 g) unsalted butter

Pomegranate seeds
Chopped parsley

METHOD

Soak the farro in a bowl of water for at least 5 hours or overnight. Don't discard the soaking liquid.

Preheat the oven to 350°F (175°C). Heat the canola oil in a Dutch oven or large ovenproof pot with a tight-fitting lid over medium-high heat. Season the short ribs on all sides with a generous amount of salt and black pepper. Sear the ribs on all sides until browned nicely, about 3 minutes per side. Transfer the short ribs to a plate. Immediately add in the onion, carrot and celery. Sweat the vegetables and stir until they've softened, about 5 minutes. Add the flour and continue cooking and stirring for another minute. Deglaze the pan with the red wine, taking care to scrape the flavor bits off the bottom. Stir in the beef stock and pomegranate molasses. Return the short ribs with any accumulated juices back to the pot and drop in the rosemary sprigs and the 2 halves of the garlic.

Bring to a boil, cover and place in the lower third of the oven. Braise for 30 minutes then turn the oven down to 300°F (150°C) for another 2 ½ hours. Remove from the oven and let cool. Once cool enough to handle, gently transfer the ribs from the sauce to a plate. If you can't manage to keep the meat on the bone, that is quite all right. Cover the ribs with tinfoil to prevent them from drying out. Strain the sauce into a measuring cup or into a fat separator. Discard the vegetables, rosemary and any bones. Spoon as much fat as possible from the top surface of the sauce and discard it. Transfer the sauce to a pot and bring to a boil over medium-high heat. Reduce the sauce by half until it's thick and almost syrupy. Taste and season accordingly with salt. It may not need it.

While the sauce is reducing, make the farrotto. Strain the farro, making sure to save 1 cup (240 ml) of soaking liquid. Bring the beef stock and water to a simmer. Heat the olive oil in a large saucepan over medium heat. Add in the onion and sauté until translucent, about 3 minutes. Stir in the farro and soaking liquid. Add the beef stock/water mixture by the ladleful, stirring often, only adding in the next ladle after almost all of the liquid has been absorbed by the farro. Continue stirring and adding liquid until the farro is cooked through. This will take about 20–25 minutes. Turn the heat off from under the farrotto and stir in the salt, pepper, heavy cream and butter. Taste and adjust seasoning.

Transfer the ribs from the plate into the reduced sauce to reheat. Spoon the sauce over to coat the meat.

Plate the farrotto on each serving dish, top with a few pieces of short ribs with a generous amount of sauce. Garnish with the pomegranate seeds and chopped parsley.

ROASTED GARLIC & APRICOT CHICKEN

"CHEEEKAN, GOOD" – LEELOO, *THE FIFTH ELEMENT*

Roasted garlic has an intoxicating smell. You can almost taste it in the air. I use roasted garlic to make a paste and smother the chicken in this dish. Letting it marinate overnight allows the flavors to penetrate the chicken, which is incredible, but my favorite part of this dish is the combination of the dried apricots and the garlicky chicken juices. Boy, oh boy.

MAKES 4 SERVINGS

INGREDIENTS

2 heads of garlic

¼ cup (6 g) chopped cilantro

¼ cup (6 g) chopped parsley

3 ½ tbsp (50 g) unsalted butter, room temp

2 tbsp (30 ml) lemon juice

1 tsp salt

½ tsp fresh black pepper

½ tsp paprika

¼ tsp cumin

½ tsp Ancho Chili Harissa (page 215), optional

8 pieces skin-on, bone-in chicken (use your favorite cuts)

¾ cup (150 g) dried apricots

1 tbsp (15 ml) olive oil

Salt and fresh black pepper

Paprika, to garnish

METHOD

Preheat oven to 375°F (190°C). Place the heads of garlic in a baking dish and roast for 40 minutes. Remove from the oven and let cool.

Cut the tops off of the heads of garlic and squeeze out the soft, sticky garlic cloves into a food processor. Add the cilantro, parsley, butter, lemon juice, salt, pepper, paprika, cumin and harissa. Pulse a few times until a thick paste has formed.

Place the chicken in a baking dish and smother with the roasted garlic paste, making sure to push some of the paste under the skin of the chicken. Cover with plastic wrap and place in the fridge to marinate overnight (or a minimum of 6 hours).

Preheat the oven to 400°F (205°C). Remove the chicken from the fridge and allow it to rest on the countertop for 15 minutes while the oven preheats. Scatter the apricots around the chicken. Drizzle with the olive oil and season with salt and pepper. Cover the top of the dish with tinfoil.

Roast for 30 minutes. Remove the tinfoil and continue roasting for an additional 15–20 minutes. The internal temperature of the chicken should reach 165°F (75°C).

Turn the broiler to high. Sprinkle the chicken with a bit of paprika and leave under the broiler to crisp for about 5 minutes or until the skin is golden brown.

Let the chicken rest for at least 5 minutes before serving.

SWEET SHREDDED HONEY LAMB

OVER COUSCOUS WITH RAISINS AND ALMONDS

Honey and lamb go hand in hand. I use ras al hanut in this recipe but instead of having you go out to try to find this fairly rare spice blend, I've broken it down so you can use the spices you already have. Marinating the lamb allows those spices to penetrate the meat. It's not very traditional to shred it, but I really like the idea of taking the work out of slicing a large piece of lamb. Placing the shredded lamb back into the sauce coats every inch of it with sticky sweetness, too. It's a win-win, really.

MAKES 6 SERVINGS

INGREDIENTS

1 trimmed 4 lb (1.8 kg) boneless leg of lamb, tied as a roast

2 cups (480 ml) water

1 tsp salt

½ tsp paprika

½ tsp ground ginger

½ tsp turmeric

½ tsp cardamom

½ tsp cinnamon

½ tsp coriander

¼ tsp cumin

¼ tsp pepper

Pinch of cloves

Pinch of nutmeg

1 tbsp (15 ml) canola oil

1 large yellow onion, grated

¾ cup (120 g) raisins

¾ cup (90 g) slivered almonds

⅓ cup (80 ml) honey

1 ½ cups (360 ml) couscous

3 tbsp (42 g) unsalted butter

½ tsp salt

1 ½ cups (360 ml) boiling water

2 tbsp (3 g) chopped parsley

METHOD

Place the tied lamb into a zip-top bag and place the bag into a deep bowl. Combine the water with all the spices and pour it over the lamb. Seal the bag and marinate it in the fridge for at least 6 hours or overnight.

Preheat the oven to 300°F (150°C). Remove the lamb from the marinade. Do not discard the marinade! Pat the lamb dry and season generously with salt and pepper.

Heat the canola oil in a Dutch oven over medium-high heat. Sear the lamb on all sides until nicely browned, about 4–5 minutes per side. Transfer the lamb to a plate. Add the grated onion to the pot. Stir and cook for 3 minutes to soften the onion. Add the lamb back into the pot with any accumulated juices. Add the raisins and pour the marinade over the lamb. Add enough water to *just* cover the lamb. Bring to a boil, cover and braise in the lower third of the oven for 3 hours. Remove from the oven and let cool.

Toast the almonds in a dry pan over medium heat, tossing, until golden, about 2 minutes. Set aside.

Once cool enough to handle, gently transfer the lamb to a plate and cover with tinfoil. Skim off as much as possible of the fat that has accumulated on the surface of the sauce using a spoon or fat separator. Stir in the honey and almonds and bring the sauce to a simmer over medium heat. Reduce until the sauce is thick. Taste for seasoning and adjust with salt if needed.

Remove the butcher's twine from the lamb and shred the meat using your hands or two forks. Discard any fat, tendons or cartilage that wouldn't be palatable. Fold the shredded lamb back into the sauce.

Place the couscous in a large heatproof bowl along with the butter and salt. Cover with the boiling water and cover with plastic wrap immediately. Let the couscous absorb the water for 5 minutes. Fluff the couscous and stir in the chopped parsley.

Plate the couscous on the serving dishes, top with the shredded lamb and sauce. Garnish with chopped parsley.

HUMMUS

WITH SAUTEED SPINACH AND RADISH SALAD

There is nothing like homemade hummus. It's better than any hummus you'll have unless you're in Israel at a place that specializes in hummus. That will probably be better. Listen, I know you can make this in five minutes using a can of chickpeas. Don't. This recipe for hummus is labor intensive. You cannot get these results from a can. Sorry—I'm not sorry. I kept this recipe vegetarian even though topping your hummus with kebabs and spiced ground beef is stupid good. This can keep in the fridge. That being said, it will start to ferment immediately and give you gas. If you don't mind gas . . . then be my guest and keep it in the fridge for a day at most.

MAKES 4 SERVINGS

INGREDIENTS

1 ½ cups (330 g) dried chickpeas

1 tsp baking soda

¾ cup (180 ml) sesame paste

2 tbsp (30 ml) lemon juice

½ tsp salt

¼ tsp cumin

2 radishes, julienned finely

1 tbsp (1.5 g) chopped parsley

1 tsp olive oil

½ tsp sumac

Pinch of salt

1 ½ tbsp (22 ml) olive oil

5 oz (140 g) spinach

1 tbsp (15 ml) lemon juice

Salt

Pinch cumin

Salt and fresh black pepper

Olive oil

Grilled pita

METHOD

Soak the chickpeas in a bowl of water for 12 to 15 hours, changing the water at least once, no earlier than 3 hours into the soak.

Drain the chickpeas and place in a large pot of water over high heat. Bring the water to a boil and cook for 2 minutes. Drain the chickpeas and rinse off the foamy "dirty" water. Return them to the pot and cover with water at least 3 inches (7.5 cm) above the chickpeas. Stir in the baking soda. Bring the water to a boil again, then turn the heat down to low and simmer for 1–1 ½ hours, uncovered, skimming any foam that comes to the top, adding a little water if needed. There should always be about 1 inch (2.5 cm) of water above the chickpeas. Turn the heat off and let the water and beans come to room temperature.

Reserve a cup (240 ml) of the cooking liquid. Drain the chickpeas. Place 2 cups (272 g) of chickpeas in a food processor, reserving the remaining beans to use for topping the hummus. Process the chickpeas until a thick paste forms. Add the sesame paste, lemon juice, salt and cumin to the food processor along with ¼ cup (60 ml) of the cooking liquid and process until super smooth. You may need to add an additional tablespoon (15 ml) of cooking liquid depending on the thickness of your hummus. Taste and adjust salt and lemon juice content accordingly to your taste. *This hummus will not be as thick as the kind you get at the store. It isn't meant to be!*

Toss together the radishes, parsley, olive oil, sumac and salt. Set aside.

Heat the olive oil in a large sauté pan over medium heat. Add all the spinach and sauté for 1–2 minutes until the spinach is just wilted. Drizzle the lemon juice over the spinach and season with a bit of salt, toss twice and remove from the pan onto a plate. Return the pan to the heat and add the reserved chickpeas. Toss to warm through. Season with cumin, salt and fresh pepper to taste. Remove the pan from the heat.

Plate the hummus, always done family style. Make a well in the middle of the hummus as best you can and add in the sautéed spinach and chickpeas and top with the radish salad. Drizzle with olive oil and serve with grilled pita.

BEER-BRAISED HOLIDAY BRISKET

WITH PRUNES OVER CREAMY GRITS

On any given Jewish holiday, boring brisket is on the menu. Jews don't feel like it's an actual holiday without it. But why does it have to be the same every single time? I'm over the basic brisket that's sliced and swimming in a flatly flavored sauce that barely sticks to the meat. Oh . . . and the carrots. No one wants those mushy carrots. I'm sorry if I have offended anyone's brisket. But if you have taken a stand on this issue and said, "No more boring brisket this Rosh Hashanah!" welcome to the club. Also, grits.

MAKES 6 SERVINGS

INGREDIENTS

2 tbsp (30 ml) canola oil

3 lb (1.3 kg) beef brisket

Salt and freshly ground pepper

1 large onion, sliced

4 cloves garlic, crushed

½ tbsp (4 g) paprika

¼ tsp turmeric

2 (12-oz [355-ml]) bottles of Goldstar beer or other amber lager such as Brooklyn Lager

½ cup (88 g) pitted prunes

1 cup (190 g) stone-ground white grits

1 tsp salt

1 ½ (360 ml) heavy cream (35%–40%)

2 ½ cups (600 ml) water

2 tbsp (28 g) unsalted butter

METHOD

Preheat the oven to 325°F (160°C).

Heat the canola oil in a large Dutch oven over medium-high heat. Generously season the brisket with salt and pepper on both sides. Sear the brisket for 5–6 minutes on each side. Transfer the brisket to a plate and add the onions to the pot. Stir and cook for 5 minutes until they have softened and picked up some color. Stir in the garlic, paprika and turmeric. Cook for another minute to release the flavors. Deglaze with 1 of the bottles of beer, scraping the bottom of the pot to release any flavor bits. Return the brisket to the pot with any accumulated juices. Top with the second bottle of beer and bring to a boil. The brisket doesn't need to be fully submerged. Add in the prunes.

Place in the lower third of the oven to braise for 3 hours, turning the brisket halfway through. Let cool slightly.

To make the grits, combine the grits, salt, heavy cream, water and butter in a sauce pot. Bring to a boil over high heat, cover and then turn the heat down to low and simmer for 10–15 minutes (depends on the brand), stirring often. Keep covered until you're ready to plate. If it becomes too thick, thin the grits with a bit of heavy cream. Taste and adjust seasoning with salt.

Carefully transfer the brisket to a plate and cover with tinfoil. Strain the sauce, reserving the onions and prunes to top the brisket. Skim off as much as possible of the fat that has accumulated at the surface of the sauce with a spoon and discard.

Bring the sauce to a simmer over medium heat and reduce to intensify the flavors. This will be more like an au jus, so do not reduce it until it is a syrup.

Plate this family style on a large cutting board. Place the grits on the board and then the brisket. Top the brisket with the onions and prunes. Drizzle a generous amount of sauce over the brisket and serve the extra sauce on the side. Slice into the brisket against the grain.

CHICKEN & BUCATINI HAMIN

SO LOW AND SO SLOW

Hamin, or *cholent*, is a type of dish that Jews make the day prior to Shabbat, since Shabbat doesn't allow for cooking. Hamin sits in the oven overnight to be eaten the next day. Normally made with large pieces of meat, potatoes, grains and lots of beans, hamin is a *Game of Thrones* type of food. Here, I've made a different type of hamin with chicken and thick bucatini. And I completely stray away from tradition when I throw in some white wine. I've changed the technique to perfect the flavor and textures of all the components. My favorite part is the bottom layer of potatoes, which becomes so creamy.

MAKES 6–8 SERVINGS

INGREDIENTS

3 white potatoes, peeled, sliced ½ inch (12 mm) thick

2 tbsp (30 ml) canola oil

8–10 pieces skin-on, bone-in chicken (thighs, legs, breast)

Salt and fresh black pepper

1 large onion, diced

1 ½ tbsp (11 g) paprika

1 cup (240 ml) white wine

1 cup (240 ml) chicken stock

1 lb (454 g) bucatini or fettuccini, broken in half

1 ½ tsp (9 g) salt

Olive oil

Salt and fresh black pepper

Paprika

METHOD

Preheat the oven to 180˚F (82˚C).

Line the bottom of an oval roaster, or large pot with tight-fitting lid, with 1 layer of potato slices and set aside the rest of the potatoes.

In a large sauté pan, heat the canola oil over medium-high heat. Season the chicken pieces with salt and fresh black pepper. In batches, sear the chicken, skin side down first, until golden brown and crispy, 7–8 minutes per side. The chicken will release from the pan when it's ready! Transfer the chicken to a plate.

Add the onion into the hot pan and sauté until translucent, about 3 minutes. Stir in the paprika and continue cooking for 1 more minute. Deglaze the pan with the white wine, scraping the bottom of the pan for any flavor bits. Stir in the stock and bring to a boil. As soon as this has come up to a boil, add in the bucatini and salt, stirring as best you can to ensure the pasta doesn't stick to itself or the pan. Boil the pasta for about 6–7 minutes until the bucatini just starts to give.

Transfer the bucatini with the liquid and the onion onto the potatoes in the roaster. Top the bucatini with the pieces of chicken. Top the chicken with another layer of potatoes. Drizzle with olive oil and season with salt, pepper and paprika. Cover and roast in the oven for 8–12 hours.

HAWAIJ OXTAIL RAGU

OVER HOMEMADE PAPPARDELLE

Hawaij (ha-wa-yej): A super ugly name for a delicious combination of spices used widely in Middle Eastern cuisine, especially by Yemenite Jews. It's got a distinct flavor that is normally used to spice soups and stews. I believe that it's even better used as a spice for ragu sauce and homemade pappardelle. If you can find hawaij, trade out the cumin, turmeric, coriander, cardamom and cloves for one to two tablespoons of it.

MAKES 6–8 SERVINGS

INGREDIENTS

3 tbsp (45 ml) canola oil

2 ½ lb (1.1 kg) oxtail

Salt and fresh black pepper

1 large yellow onion, diced

1 medium carrot, cut into ½-inch (12-mm) cubes

1 medium parsnip, cut into ½-inch (12-mm) cubes

1 small celeriac root, chopped finely

1 ½ tsp (4 g) cumin

1 tsp salt

1 tsp paprika

1 tsp turmeric

½ tsp fresh black pepper

¼ tsp coriander

Pinch of cardamom

Pinch of cloves

¼ cup (60 ml) white wine

PAPPARDELLE

1 cup (125 g) all-purpose flour

½ tsp salt

1 large egg

2 egg yolks

½ tbsp (8 ml) olive oil

2 tbsp (28 g) unsalted butter

1 tbsp (15 ml) olive oil

5 oz (140 g) baby bella mushrooms, sliced

Chopped parsley

METHOD

Preheat the oven to 275°F (135°C). Heat the canola oil in a large Dutch oven over medium-high heat. Season the oxtail with salt and fresh black pepper. Sear for 3–4 minutes on each side until browned nicely. Transfer the oxtail to a plate and set aside. Add the onion, carrots, parsnip and celeriac to the pot. Stir and cook for 5 minutes until the vegetables have softened slightly. Stir in the cumin, salt, paprika, turmeric, pepper, coriander, cardamom and cloves. Cook for a minute to release the flavors of the spices. Deglaze the pan with the white wine, scraping the bottom to release any flavor bits. Return the oxtail to the pot with just enough water to come ¾ of the way up the oxtail. Bring to a boil, cover and place in the bottom third of the oven. Braise for 3 ½–4 hours, turning the oxtail once during cooking, until the meat is falling off the bone. Set aside to cool.

To make the pappardelle, place the flour and salt in a food processor and pulse until combined and the flour is finer. Add the egg, yolks and olive oil and pulse until the dough forms a ball of sorts. If the dough is too dry, add a teaspoon more of olive oil and pulse again. Remove the dough from the processor and lightly knead it into a tight ball. Cover with two layers of plastic wrap and let it rest for 40 minutes. Then, cut the dough into 4 equal portions. Working in batches, roll the dough in a pasta machine dusted with flour. When you're not working with any pasta dough, rolled or not, keep it covered with a kitchen towel to prevent it from drying out. Roll the dough thin enough to see your hand through it.

Fold each pasta sheet into thirds and cut the folded sheet into 1-inch- (2.5-cm)-wide noodles and set aside on flour-dusted sheet pan. Cover with a kitchen towel.

Once the oxtail is cool enough to handle, remove the pieces from the sauce. Remove the meat from the bone and discard the bone. Return the oxtail meat to the sauce. Then, bring a large pot of salted water to a boil and heat a large sauté pan with the butter and olive oil over medium heat. Sauté the mushrooms, making sure not to crowd the pan, for 2 minutes. Do this in batches if you need. Combine the mushrooms with the oxtail ragu in the sauté pan and warm the sauce through. While the ragu is warming, cook the pappardelle in the boiling water until al dente, 4–5 minutes. Reserve ½ cup (120 ml) of the cooking liquid, drain the pasta and transfer it immediately to the ragu. Toss the sauce and pasta together adding a bit of pasta cooking liquid if the sauce seems too thick.

Plate the pappardelle family style on a large platter and garnish with chopped parsley.

CURRY LAMB CHOPS

WITH OKRA & FINGERLING POTATOES

This is what an Israeli would call a "curry." It's a stew of sorts with a ton of spices (as usual) and some whole vegetables. Okra, or *bamye*, is abundant in Israeli cooking. I have my own personal feelings about the texture of okra, but once I can get past it, I do love the taste. I use loin chops in this recipe even though it's a cut you can easily grill and eat in less than 10 minutes. I just enjoy eating handheld cuts of meat off the bone. You can also use a shoulder chop if you want some extra meat. The idea is to have both bone and meat for the flavor development of this dish.

MAKES 4 SERVINGS

INGREDIENTS

3 tbsp (45 ml) canola oil

1 large onion, diced

4 cloves garlic, sliced thinly

2 tsp (4 g) turmeric

1 tsp salt

½ tsp cumin

½ tsp yellow curry

8 pieces lamb loin chops

¾ lb (340 g) okra, tops removed

½ lb (227 g) fingerling potatoes

Chopped parsley

METHOD

In a large sauté pan with tight-fitting lid, heat the oil over medium heat. Sauté the onion for 4 minutes until softened. Stir in the garlic, turmeric, salt, cumin and yellow curry. Cook and stir for an additional minute to release the flavors. Arrange the loin chops, okra and potatoes in the pan. Add enough water to come ¾ of the way up the lamb. Bring to a boil, cover, turn down the heat to low. Simmer for 2 ½ hours until the vegetables are tender.

Slice the potatoes into ¼-inch (6-mm) rounds. Plate the okra on each serving dish along with two pieces of lamb chops. Lay the potatoes around the chops and drizzle a bit of sauce onto the chops and vegetables. Garnish with chopped parsley.

PASTRAMI

IN A SANDWICH WITH MUSTARDAH

When I say pastrami, I'm taken back to Katz's, Carnegie and those foggy New York deli windows. If you search in Israel for pastrami, you won't find a whole lot. I think all the Eastern European Jews moved to New York and brought the pastrami with them. I feel like it's making a comeback. For the longest time, I've been saying that the Reuben is making a comeback. I'm hedging my bets, but be on the lookout. This recipe is not very labor intensive but takes patience. You can make a ton of it. It will keep in the fridge to make sandwiches for days! Or a Reuben hash with poached egg, found on page 119.

MAKES ABOUT 3 POUNDS (1.3 KILOS) OF PASTRAMI

INGREDIENTS

BRINE

3 ½ quarts (3.3 L) water

5 cloves garlic, crushed

¾ cup (240 g) coarse kosher salt (use the weight amount)

½ cup (100 g) sugar

½ cup (110 g) dark brown sugar

3 tbsp (45 ml) honey

3 tbsp (12 g) pickling spice

2 tbsp (35 g) pink curing salt

1 tbsp (11 g) yellow mustard seeds

1 tbsp (15 ml) liquid smoke

3 lb (1.3 kg) beef brisket

SPICES

3 tbsp (23 g) coriander seeds

2 ½ tbsp (28 g) yellow mustard seeds

1 ½ tbsp (12 g) black peppercorns

1 tbsp (7 g) paprika

SANDWICH

Pastrami

Brown mustard, or other good-quality mustard

Rye bread slices

METHOD

I highly recommend using the weight measurements when following this recipe.

Bring the brine mixture to a boil and then let it come to room temperature *completely*. Place the brisket in the brine and let it sit in the fridge, untouched, for 5 to 7 days. Don't try to rush this process.

Remove the brisket from the brine and rinse. Pat it dry with paper towel. Lay it on a baking sheet and allow it to air-dry for an hour.

Preheat the oven to 225°F (105°C).

In a dry pan, toast the coriander seeds, mustard seeds and peppercorn for 3 minutes until fragrant and they begin to pop. Transfer them to a bowl and grind with a mortar and pestle, in batches, leaving the mix fairly coarse. You can also do this in a spice grinder; just be cautious not to grind the mixture too finely. Combine the crushed seeds with the paprika and press the mixture onto the brisket, taking care to cover it entirely.

Pour about an inch (2.5 cm) of boiling water at the bottom of a roasting pan with a wire rack. The water should be below the rack. Place the crusted brisket on top of the rack and cover with the lid or tent the roasting pan tightly with two layers of heavy-duty tinfoil. You do not want any moisture to escape. Roast the brisket for no less than 6 hours and up to 10 hours.

Remove the roasting pan from the oven and let it rest for at least an hour before removing the lid.

Remove the pastrami from the roasting pan and let it rest on a cutting board for 15 minutes before slicing into it.

This will keep in the fridge for up to 1 week, in an airtight container or wrapped very well in plastic wrap. The pastrami will be easier to slice if it is cold out of the fridge.

Slice the pastrami against the grain as thinly as possible without crumbling the meat. This is easier if the meat has been refrigerated.

Steam the sliced meat to warm it through and keep it juicy.

Spread a very generous amount of mustard on both sides of the rye. Top with the warmed meat. Close your eyes. Thank the meat gods.

BRUNCH

THE BEST MEAL OF THE WEEK

Brunch should be the biggest meal of the week: coffee and cocktails, eggs on everything. Eat a lot since you have the rest of the day to digest. Take the time to make brunch, unlike a breakfast on the go. I've taken Israeli flavors and fused them with my brunch favorites. For example, instead of using basic red tomatoes for a classic *shakshuka* dish, I've pulled from Mexican cuisine and used tomatillos. I think that's pretty genius. If I could have made the whole book about brunch, I probably would have. Israelis love a family-style brunch, sharing food and germs alike.

ROASTED TOMATILLO & POBLANO SHAKSHUKA

GREEN EGGS. HOLD THE HAM.

Remember that leftover challah from Friday night? Pull it out along with every other carb in the house. This is the ultimate family-style brunch dish. You'll find so many versions of this dish all over Israel and now, the United States. Every blogger is making it, and there's a reason for it: IT'S THE BEST BRUNCH DISH ON EARTH. If you break it down, shakshuka is a dish of eggs poached in (usually) a spiced tomato sauce. This version is made with a few changes to the classic-style shakshuka. The main difference is that I use tomatillos instead of tomatoes, which makes the whole thing green instead of red. I char them under the broiler with a poblano pepper to give more flavor depth in a matter of minutes. This will become a favorite of yours.

MAKES 3–4 SERVINGS

INGREDIENTS

1 large poblano pepper

8 medium tomatillos, husks removed

3 cloves garlic

½ cup (12 g) cilantro

1 ½ tbsp (23 ml) olive oil

½ tsp salt

¼ tsp cumin

2 long hot peppers

4 eggs

Za'atar

Chopped cilantro

Grilled pita

METHOD

Place a rack at the top third of the oven and turn the broiler on to high.

Line a baking sheet with tinfoil. Place the poblano on the baking sheet and broil for 13–15 minutes, turning it to get a good char all around the pepper. Transfer the pepper to a cutting board. Place the tomatillos on the baking sheet and place them under the broiler for 7–8 minutes, turning to get a good char on both tops and bottoms of the tomatillos.

Transfer the tomatillos and any accumulated juices into a blender. Remove the stem from the poblano and discard it. Transfer the poblano to the blender along with the garlic and cilantro. Blend on high until pureed.

Heat the olive oil in the largest skillet or sauté pan with a lid that you own over medium-low heat. Add the tomatillo mixture into the pan. Stir in the salt and cumin and bring up to a simmer. Lay the long hot peppers in the sauce and turn the heat down to low. Cover the skillet and simmer for 10 minutes, stirring occasionally.

Turn the heat up to medium. Create, as best you can, pockets inside the sauce and crack an egg into each one. If you can fit more than 4 eggs in your pan, please do, but do not crowd the eggs. There should be sauce between the eggs to help them simmer properly! Immediately cover the pan and cook, undisturbed, for 2–2 ½ minutes until the whites of the eggs have *just* set.

Garnish with za'atar and chopped cilantro. Remove the pan from the heat and serve immediately with grilled pita.

ZUCCHINI LATKES EGGS BENNIE

WITH DILL LABANE SAUCE

Christmukkah Brunch 2011: I had four friends peeling and grating potatoes for latkes. Had one grating only onions, poor thing. That is what this dish reminds me of. Good times and friends and latkes. Don't wait 'til next Hanukkah to make these, though! Make it this weekend! Fried things are tasty all year round. Making the latkes with zucchini instead of potatoes gives the dish more freshness and color. The flavor combination of the zucchini latkes, salmon, egg yolk and dill labane sauce works so perfectly together.

MAKES 4 SERVINGS

INGREDIENTS

1 cup (250 g) Labane (page 219) or Greek yogurt

⅓ cup (80 ml) water

1 tsp chopped dill

1 tsp lemon juice

Pinch of salt

1 large or 2 small zucchinis, grated

Canola oil for frying

2 tbsp (16 g) all-purpose flour

1 large egg

½ tsp chopped dill

¼ tsp salt

Fresh ground pepper

4 oz (110 g) smoked nova salmon

4 poached eggs

Chopped chives

4 lemon wedges

METHOD

To make the dill labane sauce, combine the labane, water, dill, lemon juice and salt; cover and set in the fridge until ready to serve.

Place the grated zucchini inside of a sheet of cheesecloth and wring out as much water as possible without destroying the zucchini.

Heat a skillet with ¼ inch (6 mm) of oil over medium-low heat. Just before frying the latkes, combine the drained zucchini, flour, egg, dill, salt and fresh pepper to taste in a bowl and form them into 4 patties. Fry for 2 minutes on each side until golden brown. Transfer the latkes to a paper-towel-lined plate. Sprinkle with some salt.

Plate the latkes on each serving dish, top with the smoked salmon and poached egg. Garnish with chopped chives and serve with a lemon wedge.

MUSHROOM & CARAMELIZED ONION BOUREKAS

BIG IS BETTER

Bourekas are a form of puff-pastry pockets filled with anything from cheeses and spinach to meat and potatoes. There are bakeries that specialize in these. Normally they are a handheld grab-and-go breakfast for Israelis, but I've decided they need to be massive. Like really, really big. Each one of these can feed two people. If you must, make them smaller by using small squares of puff pastry instead of large ones. You just won't be as cool as I thought you could be. The cheesy potato and caramelized onion mixture is perfect eaten on its own, but when you top it with sautéed mushrooms and enclose it in buttery, flaky puff pastry, it's like you've died and gone to heaven.

MAKES 4 SERVINGS

INGREDIENTS

½ tbsp (8 ml) olive oil

1 ½ tbsp (21 g) unsalted butter

1 large yellow onion, sliced

Pinch salt

1 large white potato, peeled and quartered

¼ cup (30 g) grated *kashkaval* or provolone cheese

1 egg yolk

¼ tsp salt

Fresh black pepper

½ tbsp (8 ml) olive oil

½ tbsp (7 g) unsalted butter

4 oz (110 g) baby bella mushrooms, sliced

Salt and fresh black pepper

1 egg

2 sheets store bought puff pastry, thawed in the fridge overnight

Sesame seeds

Maldon salt

Fresh black pepper

Cucumber slices

Hard-boiled egg slices

METHOD

For the caramelized onions, heat the olive oil and butter over low heat in a large sauté pan with lid. Add the sliced onion, sprinkle with the salt and cover. Cook, covered, for about 25 minutes, stirring every so often. Remove the lid, turn the heat up to medium and continue cooking, stirring often for another 10 to 15 minutes. The onion will become a deep caramel color. It may need an additional 5 to 10 minutes to get to its deepest color. This takes time. Do not rush it! Turn the heat off when you've achieved the desired caramelization. Set aside.

For the potato filling, bring a pot of water to a boil with the potato already in it. Boil until the potato is fork tender, 8 to 12 minutes depending on the size of the potato. Remove the potato from the water and immediately push it through a ricer. You can also mash it by hand. Combine the mashed potato with the *kashkaval*, egg yolk, salt and fresh black pepper to taste.

Combine the caramelized onion with the mashed potatoes. Set aside.

For the mushrooms, heat a large sauté pan with the olive oil and butter over medium heat. Sauté the mushrooms, making sure not to crowd the pan, for 2 minutes. Do this in batches if needed. Season with salt and pepper to taste. Set aside.

Preheat the oven to 375°F (190°C) and line a baking sheet with parchment paper. Prepare the egg wash by whisking the egg with a splash of water.

Right out of the fridge, unroll the puff pastry onto a lightly floured surface. Cut the sheets down to two 8-inch (20-cm) squares. Transfer the sheets to the prepared baking sheet. Fill each with the potato and onion mixture in the middle, taking care to leave at least a ½ inch (12 mm) border. Top the potato mix with the mushrooms. Brush the egg wash along all 4 edges of the puff pastry and fold into a diamond shape, sealing along all the edges. Crimp the edges with a fork to ensure that the pockets have sealed.

Brush the bourekas with the egg wash generously. Sprinkle with the sesame seeds, Maldon salt and fresh black pepper. Bake for 32 to 35 minutes until perfectly golden brown and fully puffed.

Serve with cucumber slices and hard-boiled eggs seasoned with salt and fresh pepper.

CHOCOLATE BABKA FRENCH TOAST

WITH FRESH WHIP AND PISTACHIOS

Babka has become a fad. But in reality, it's been a bread delicacy for many a year. It's made from a yeasty bread dough that is rolled with chocolate, poppy seeds or cinnamon, then split in half and braided for the ultimate swirled bread. If you make this at home, more power to you. Store-bought babka is great and when you can buy it from the store, you don't have to make it (unless you work at that store). So instead of a boring challah French toast, we're going babka on it. Be ready for a sugar high and then a sugar crash. But a happy sugar crash nonetheless.

MAKES 4 SERVINGS

INGREDIENTS

1 loaf chocolate babka

1 cup (240 ml) heavy cream (35%-40%)

1 cup (240 ml) milk

6 large eggs

1 ½ tbsp (23 ml) vanilla bean paste, or extract

½ tsp salt

1 cup (240 ml) heavy whipping cream (35%-50%)

3 tbsp (40 g) sugar

½ tsp vanilla bean paste or extract

Butter for frying

Powdered sugar

Chopped pistachios

Maple syrup

METHOD

Slice the babka into 8 thick slices. The slices will be fragile so take care when moving them around.

Whisk together the heavy cream, milk, eggs, vanilla bean paste and salt in a large baking dish.

To make the whipped cream, whisk together the heavy cream, sugar and vanilla bean paste in a cold metal bowl until soft peaks form.

Preheat the oven to 180°F (85°C). And prepare a baking sheet with cooling rack.

Heat a few tablespoons (about 28 g) of butter in a large frying pan or griddle over medium-low heat. Do these next steps in batches depending on how many slices you can fit in your pan. Soak the slices of babka in the custard for 15 seconds on each side and place straight into the pan. Cook for 3-4 minutes on each side. Transfer the French toast onto a cooling rack and into the oven to keep warm while you finish making the rest of the French toast. Add more butter to the pan with each new batch.

When ready to serve, plate 2 pieces of French toast on each serving dish and dust lightly with powdered sugar. Garnish with chopped pistachios and whipped cream. Serve with maple syrup.

SLOW-ROASTED SALMON PLATTER

WITH ALL THE FIXINGS FOR A BAR MITZVAH BRUNCH

Ever been to one of those Jewish lunch-ins or bar mitzvah brunches? Yes? So you know they serve bagels, smear and smoked salmon. That spread is a very Jewish-American idea of brunch. This is my take on that classic spread that Israeli Jews in the States giggle about behind everyone's back. It's easy to make ahead too, which is always a bonus if you're having friends or family over for a brunch and you're still hungover from the night before.

MAKES 4–6 SERVINGS

INGREDIENTS

1 ½ lb (680 g) sushi-grade salmon fillet

½ tbsp (8 ml) olive oil

½ tbsp (8 ml) lemon juice

½ tbsp (9 g) grainy mustard

Salt and fresh pepper

1 lemon, sliced thinly

Olive oil

4 bagels, sliced into thirds

Salt and fresh black pepper

8 oz (225 g) cream cheese or Labane (page 219)

Avocado, thinly sliced

Sumac

Cucumber, thinly sliced

Radish, thinly sliced

Red onion, thinly sliced

Chopped chives

Capers

Lemon wedges

Maldon salt

METHOD

Preheat the oven to 200°F (95°C).

Place the salmon fillet on a lightly greased baking sheet. Combine the olive oil, lemon juice and mustard. Spoon the mustard mixture over and around the salmon. Season with salt and fresh pepper and arrange the lemon slices on top of the salmon in a decorative way.

Roast in the middle rack of the oven for 50 minutes to 1 hour. Remove from the oven and let cool. Wrap the baking sheet tightly and place it in the fridge for at least 3 hours and no more than 12 hours.

Drizzle the olive oil on both sides of each bagel slice and season generously with salt and pepper. Grill on high for a minute or two on each side. You can also use a panini press to achieve more of a bagel chip feel.

Transfer the salmon onto the serving platter carefully. Arrange the bagels and the fixings around the salmon. Season all the vegetables with a bit of Maldon salt and garnish the cream cheese and avocado with sumac.

REUBEN HASH SKILLET

JUST LIKE THE SANDWICH

Hungover? Again? This is the cure. Everything you want in a Reuben, but in a breakfast skillet. You made that pastrami, I hope (page 106). If not, store-bought will do. The potatoes are creamy and soft in the middle with a nice crisp edge on the outside. The eggs are runny. The Swiss is melty. The pastrami is meaty. The sauerkraut is . . . well . . . sour. Fantastic combination and, of course, eaten family style.

MAKES 4 SERVINGS

INGREDIENTS

1 large russet potato, cut into 1-inch (2.5-cm) pieces

2 tbsp (30 ml) olive oil

¼ tsp salt

2 pinches paprika

Fresh black pepper

⅓ lb (150 g) shredded pastrami meat

½ cup (80 g) sauerkraut

¼ cup (30 g) shredded Swiss cheese

4 eggs

Salt and fresh black pepper

METHOD

Bring a large pot of water to a boil. Drop the potatoes in and cook until *just* fork tender, about 6–7 minutes. Drain and return the potatoes to the pot to dry out in the residual heat.

In a large skillet, heat the olive oil over medium-high heat. Add in the potatoes, salt, paprika and fresh black pepper to taste. Toss to coat the potatoes in the oil and spices. Let the potatoes cook, untouched, for at least 4 minutes. Toss and then continue cooking, undisturbed, for an additional 4 minutes. This will allow a crust to form on the potatoes.

Once the potatoes are crispy, add in the pastrami and sauerkraut. Toss to mix with the potatoes. Sprinkle the shredded cheese over top. Make pockets in the potatoes for the eggs to sit in and crack the eggs into the pockets. Immediately cover and allow to cook for 2–2 ½ minutes until the whites are just set and the yolks are still runny.

Season with salt and fresh pepper.

ZA'ATAR SESAME MINI BAGELS

JERSEY MEETS JAFFA

In our universe, there are bagels with big holes, there are bagels with small holes and there are bagels with buttholes—those bagels that are so doughy and puffy that their hole basically closes up. These are somewhere inbetween. Za'atar is a combination of spices that has been used in the Middle East for centuries. It's nutty and a little woodsy. It works so well with a chunky, carby bagel. I make sure to really get a great covering of it onto the bagel to really get the hit of the spice.

MAKES 14 MINI BAGELS

INGREDIENTS

1 ⅓ cup (195 g) bread flour

1 ¾ tsp (8 g) dry active yeast, one packet

1 cup (240 ml) warm water

3 cups (375 g) all-purpose flour

1 tbsp (11 g) dark brown sugar

¼ cup (60 ml) olive oil

1 large egg

1 tbsp (20 g) kosher salt

¼ cup (55 g) sesame seeds

¼ cup (36 g) za'atar

2 tbsp (18 g) Maldon salt

1 tbsp (21 g) baking soda

METHOD

In the bowl of a stand mixer, whisk together, by hand, the bread flour, yeast and water. Cover with damp towel and leave in a warm place to rise for 1 hour.

Add the flour, brown sugar, olive oil, egg and salt to the "mother" and mix on low with a dough hook attachment for 2 minutes until the dough is combined. Turn the mixer up to medium-low and let the machine knead the dough for 6 minutes. Alternatively, you can knead for 10 minutes by hand on a lightly floured surface.

Transfer the dough to a lightly oiled bowl. Cover with damp towel and leave in a warm place to rise for 2 hours until the dough has doubled in size.

Prepare 2 baking sheets lined with tinfoil and lightly spray them with cooking oil.

Divide the dough into 14 equal portions of 65 grams each. Best way to do this is to weigh the dough and scale out portions. Form each portion into a nice tight ball by folding the dough onto itself and into the middle until you get a nice smooth top. Cup the ball in your hand with the seam side against the work surface and seal the seams by rolling it in a circular motion. Poke a hole in each of the bagels using your thumb by slowly pushing your thumb through while rotating it. I like these holes small, but feel free to make them as big or small as you like.

Place them on the 2 prepared baking sheets at least 2 inches (5 cm) apart. Cover them with a damp kitchen towel and leave them in a warm place to rise for 45 minutes to an hour until doubled in size.

Toast the sesame seeds in a dry pan over medium heat, tossing constantly, until golden brown, 3-4 minutes. Mix the sesame seeds with the za'atar and Maldon salt.

Preheat the oven to 400°F (205°F). Bring a large pot of water and the baking soda to a boil. Gently drop the bagels into the water. Do these in batches of 3-4 depending on how many will fit in your pot. Don't crowd the bagels! Boil for 2 minutes on each side. Using a slotted spoon, remove the bagels from the water and place them back on the greased baking sheet leaving at least 2 inches (5 cm) between them. As soon as they come out of the water, roll them in the topping making sure to get all sides and the bottom too. Continue with the rest of the bagels.

Place the baking sheets in the center of the oven and bake for 27–30 minutes, turning the pans halfway through, until the bagels are golden brown.

They are best eaten the day of, but not too shabby when you toast them the next day.

ROASTED BEET & LABANE EGG SANDWICH

ON PUMPERNICKEL WITH OLIVE-OIL FRIED EGG

This is just a good old beet sandwich. Hold on: Is there such a thing as a "good old beet sandwich"? Probably not. Either way, roasted beets feel super meaty when roasted and sliced. The labane and sumac are perfect accompaniments to it. And no brunch sandwich is complete without a fried egg. This one is super crispy and fried in olive oil.

MAKES 4 SERVINGS

INGREDIENTS

2 small red beets

2 small golden beets

Olive oil for frying

4 eggs

Salt and fresh black pepper

8 slices toasted pumpernickel bread, rye or marble works too

Labane (page 219)

Sumac

Salt and fresh black pepper

METHOD

Preheat the oven to 400°F (205°C). Wrap the red beets and golden beets separately in tinfoil. Roast in the oven for about 40 minutes until tender. Depending on the size of the beets, this may take a bit longer.

When the beets are cool enough to handle, rub the skin off the beets with a paper towel. It should slip right off. Slice the beets into ¼-inch- (6-mm) thick slices.

Heat about 1 ½–2 tablespoons (23–30 ml) olive oil in a medium fry pan over medium-low heat. When the oil is hot, crack the egg into the pan. The whites will immediately start to bubble. Don't crowd the pan; fry 2 eggs at most at a time. You may need to add a bit more oil between batches. Fry for 2 ½ to 3 minutes until the whites are set and the yolk is still runny. Transfer onto a paper-towel-lined plate. Season with salt and fresh pepper.

Assemble the sandwiches by spreading a good amount of labane on one half of the pumpernickel toast. Sprinkle with a sumac, salt and fresh pepper. Top with one layer of red beets and another of golden beets. Top each with a fried egg, and top the sandwich with the second slice of toast.

VANILLA MUESLI WITH TORN DATES

AND FRESH FRUIT

This is my ode to the land of milk and honey, the land of Israel. Don't move there if you are lactose-intolerant. Dairy is such a big part of the cuisine, especially for breakfast. Normally your morning meal isn't complete until you've had at least three kinds of cheeses. Before hitting the beach for an early-morning workout, I sit and have a bowl of muesli. It's basically a bowl of yogurt with oats and granola, but it comes with a fancy name. This recipe uses a technique where the oats are soaked overnight in milk. In the morning they are soft and oatmeal-like. Use whatever fresh fruit is seasonal, and if you can find Medjool dates from Israel, you will not be disappointed.

MAKES 2 SERVINGS

INGREDIENTS

1 cup (105 g) rolled oats
⅔ cup (160 ml) milk
½ tsp vanilla bean paste or extract
⅔ cup (165 g) Greek yogurt, optional
Honey
Medjool dates, torn
Bananas
Blackberries
Sliced almonds
Salted pistachios, chopped

METHOD

Combine the oats, milk and vanilla bean paste, cover and place in the fridge for 8 hours or up to 15 hours.

Mix the muesli with the Greek yogurt. This step is optional. You can eat the muesli without the yogurt as well!

Plate the muesli into the serving bowls and drizzle with honey over the top. Arrange your desired amount of torn dates, bananas, blackberries, sliced almonds and salted pistachios.

SABICH BREAKFAST BOWLS

WITH SHREDDED POTATO HASH

Normally packed in a pita, this is a traditional Iraqi Jewish Shabbat breakfast. It consists of fried eggplant and hard-boiled eggs, but then it's surrounded with tahini, *amba*, schug, Israeli salad, pickles, etc. It's an everything sandwich. I wanted to make it into a breakfast bowl, and so I did. Instead of a hard-boiled egg, a soft one takes its place. #yolkporn

MAKES 4 SERVINGS

INGREDIENTS

1 large eggplant

Coarse kosher salt

1 kirby cucumber, diced

1 Roma tomato, diced

1 tbsp (1.5 g) chopped parsley

1 tsp lemon juice

Salt to taste

4 eggs

Canola oil for frying

Salt

2 russet potatoes, peeled

1 ½ tbsp (23 ml) canola oil

½ yellow onion, sliced

Pinch paprika

Salt and fresh black pepper to taste

Tahini (page 212)

Amba, store bought or page 224

Israeli pickles, sliced

Chopped parsley

METHOD

Slice the eggplant into ½-inch- (12-mm)-thick slices. Lay them on a paper-towel-lined baking sheet. Sprinkle both sides with a generous amount of coarse kosher salt and let rest for about 10 minutes while the moisture is extracted from the eggplant.

To make the salad, toss the cucumber, tomato, parsley, lemon juice and salt and set in the fridge until ready to serve.

To make the soft-boiled eggs, bring a pot of water to a rolling boil and prepare a bowl filled with ice water. Slowly lower each egg into the water, taking care not to break them. Boil for exactly 6 minutes. Immediately remove the eggs from the boiling water and into the ice bath to shock them and stop the cooking. Leave them in the ice bath for 4 minutes. Gently and carefully peel the eggs and set aside.

Preheat the oven to 180°F (85°C). Brush away the salt from the eggplant slices. Cut them into ½-inch (12-mm) cubes.

In a large fry pan, heat ¼ inch (6 mm) of canola oil over medium heat. Fry the eggplants, turning as they brown, until golden, about 3 minutes. Drain them on a paper-towel-lined baking sheet. Do this in batches and season the eggplant with salt as soon as they come out of the oil. Remove the paper towel and set the eggplant into the oven to keep warm.

To make the potato hash, grate the potatoes. Place the grated potatoes on a few sheets of paper towel or a clean kitchen towel, pressing with another paper towel on top to remove as much of the moisture as possible from the potatoes. Really press on them.

Heat a large skillet with the canola oil over medium heat. Add in the onions and sauté for 2–3 minutes until softened. Add in the grated potatoes and toss to coat the potatoes with a bit of the oil. Season with paprika, salt and fresh black pepper to taste, and toss again. Fry for 4–5 minutes, tossing only once until golden brown and cooked through. The potatoes will stick together slightly; that is a thumbs-up.

Plate the bowls by placing the potato hash at the bottom, and top with the eggplant and Israeli salad. Drizzle a decent amount of tahini over everything. Place the soft-boiled egg on top and cut in half. Serve with amba, Israeli pickles and chopped parsley.

CARAMELIZED-ONION CHOPPED LIVER

WITH RITZ CRACKERS

This is another one of those Jewish dishes that has migrated across the ocean to the States. All the chopped liver I've had in New York is super sweet and almost pâté-like in texture. I like my chopped liver on the saltier side with a bit more texture. Why Ritz crackers, you ask? Because it's the perfect cracker—salty and buttery. The radish adds a fresh, peppery crunch that I love. Feel free to pile it high on a bagel though. Just as good.

MAKES 4 SERVINGS

INGREDIENTS

1 ½ tbsp (21 g) unsalted butter

1 tbsp (15 ml) olive oil or schmaltz

2 large yellow onions, sliced ¼-inch (6-mm) thick

Salt

1 lb (454 g) chicken liver

Salt and fresh black pepper

3 ½ tbsp (52 ml) olive oil

2 hard-boiled eggs

½ tsp salt

½ tsp fresh black pepper

1 radish, julienned finely

1 hard-boiled egg, sliced

Chopped parsley

Fresh black pepper

Ritz crackers

METHOD

For the caramelized onions, heat the olive oil and butter over low heat in a large sauté pan with lid. Add the sliced onions, sprinkle with the salt and cover. Cook, covered, for about 25 minutes, stirring every so often. Remove the lid, turn the heat up to medium and continue cooking, stirring often for another 10–15 minutes. The onions will become a deep caramel color. They may need an additional 5–10 minutes to get to their deepest color. This takes time. Do not rush it! Turn the heat off when you've achieved the desired caramelization.

Before frying the livers, clean and trim away any fat or connective tissue. Pat them dry with a paper towel to remove as much moisture as possible. Season them generously with salt and lots of black pepper. Remove the onions from the sauté pan. Heat the olive oil over medium-high heat. Add the livers and fry for 5 minutes per side. Be careful. The oil will jump. Use a splatter screen as the livers fry if you have one. Once the livers are completely cooked through, turn the heat off and let them cool in the pan.

Place the liver, along with the oil, two thirds of the caramelized onions, hard-boiled eggs, salt and pepper, in a food processor. Pulse until all the contents are finely chopped but not pureed. Taste for seasoning and adjust with salt and pepper.

Serve in a bowl topped with the remaining caramelized onions, radish and slices of hard-boiled egg and garnished with chopped parsley and fresh pepper. Place the Ritz crackers beside the bowl as an accompaniment.

COLD-BREWED MILK COFFEE

WITH COFFEE CUBES

If you're yearning for caffeine, this is more of a treat than an energy kick. In this day and age where we cold brew coffee, I thought it would be appropriate to cold brew it straight into the milk. Add some vodka and shake it up with the coffee cubes for a white Russian of sorts. Now *there* is a great idea. My favorite beach restaurant serves a version of this. I normally order it to finish off a lunch if I'm craving something cold and sweet.

MAKES 2 SERVINGS

INGREDIENTS

¼ cup (60 ml) brewed coffee

⅓ cup (28 g) coarsely ground coffee

1 ½ cups (360 ml) 2% milk

¼ cup (50 g) sugar

¼ cup (60 ml) boiling water

METHOD

Pour the brewed coffee into an ice tray to make the coffee cubes. Place in the freezer overnight.

Combine the coffee grinds with the milk in a French press and set in the fridge to steep for a minimum of 8 hours or overnight. The longer it sits, the stronger it will be.

Combine the sugar and boiling water to make the simple syrup.

Place the coffee cubes in 2 glasses. Press the plunger down all the way to the bottom of the French press to push the grinds away from the milk. Pour the cold-brewed milk coffee over the coffee cubes.

Sweeten with simple syrup to taste. As the coffee cubes melt, the drink will get more intense.

MIDNIGHT

THE CARB AND EGG CHAPTER

As always, it's late and I'm hungry. I give in. These are the snacks and mini meals that I make during those late hours when I should be keeping my chompy mouth shut. I know it's happened to you before. If you can't tell yet, I really enjoy my carbs. This chapter is dedicated to my love for them with a loud shout-out to eggs and my grill pan.

FETA GRILLED CHEESE

WITH OLIVES

A grilled cheese sandwich doesn't need much introduction. This recipe is to tell you about my love for feta cheese—especially the soft, smooth French-style feta cheese that you can just spread onto a piece of toast. That is the best kind to use for this recipe, although any feta cheese you have on hand will be just as tasty.

MAKES 1 SERVING

INGREDIENTS

2 slices sourdough bread

¼ cup (28 g) or more crumbled French-style creamy feta cheese

2 slices Havarti cheese

2 tbsp (22 g) torn kalamata olives

2 tbsp (28 g) melted butter

METHOD

Spread the feta cheese on each slice of the sourdough slices. Lay one slice of the Havarti on one of the halves. Place some torn olives on top of the Havarti slice, top with another slice of Havarti and place the other half of the sourdough with feta on top.

Heat a grill pan or panini press on medium-low heat. Brush both sides of the sandwich with a very generous amount of melted butter. Grill, placing a heavy pan on top of the sandwich to press it down, for 2–3 minutes on each side until golden brown and the cheese is melted.

ANCHOVIES WITH PRESERVED LEMON

AND PIQUILLO PEPPERS . . . ON TOAST, OBVI

Raid the pantry! That's the kind of midnight snack that requires minimal effort. I adore the flavor combo of the anchovies, preserved lemons and piquillo peppers. Such a good match. Make this for your next tapas party or as an appetizer to a dinner.

MAKES 2–4 SERVINGS

INGREDIENTS

Olive oil

4 slices country bread

Salt and fresh black pepper

2 cloves garlic, cut in half

Good-quality anchovies packed in olive oil

Piquillo peppers

Preserved Lemons (page 223), sliced thinly

Capers

Chopped parsley

Half of a lemon

METHOD

Heat a grill pan on high. Drizzle a generous amount of olive oil on each side of the slices of country bread and season generously with salt and pepper. Grill each side for a minute or two until nicely charred and golden brown. As soon as you remove the bread from the grill pan, rub both sides with the cut side of the garlic.

Dress the toast with anchovies, piquillo peppers, preserved lemon slices, capers and chopped parsley. Squeeze a bit of fresh lemon juice over top.

CACIO E PEPE

MAMA'S SPECIALTY WITH FETA CHEESE

My mom is the queen of late-night snacking. She'll fall asleep in the living room then, in a panic, wake up and walk to the kitchen, literally shoving something in her mouth as she lets us know she's going up to sleep. This is her Israeli-fied recipe for a nice twist on the classic Roman dish of *cacio e pepe*.

MAKES 2 SERVINGS

INGREDIENTS

½ lb (225 g) spaghetti

1 cup (113 g) shredded *kashkaval* or provolone cheese

½ cup (55 g) crumbled Bulgarian feta cheese

1 egg, beaten

1 tsp fresh black pepper

½ tsp salt

METHOD

Bring a large pot of salt water to a boil. Cook the pasta until al dente. Before draining the pasta, reserve ⅓ cup (80 ml) of starchy cooking liquid. Drain the pasta and return it back to the pot.

Vigorously stir in the *kashkaval*, feta, egg, pepper and salt until combined with the pasta. Add some of the pasta liquid if needed to thin the sauce a bit. You may not need it! It should form a luxurious thick cheese sauce that hugs the spaghetti. Check seasoning and serve.

EGGS AND SUMAC SOLDIERS

PULL OUT THOSE EGG CUPS, FINALLY

If my memory serves me correctly, my grandpa had a soft-boiled egg almost every day. My brother and I used to conspire with my grandma and play the same joke on him each time he sat down for his egg. Before he arrived at the table, we would finish our own eggs and then serve our upside-down empty shell to him. He would use his spoon to crack the top off his egg and to his "surprise" the egg would be empty! Classic. Without fail, he would play along, each and every time. The sumac toast is super buttery and slightly tangy from the sumac. Dipping it into the runny yolk adds the perfect creamy flavor to it. You'll never have eggs and soldiers any other way.

MAKES 2 SERVINGS

INGREDIENTS

3 tbsp (42 g) unsalted butter, softened

1 tsp sumac

Salt

2 slices white bread

2–4 eggs

Salt and fresh black pepper

METHOD

Combine the softened butter, sumac and a pinch of salt in a small bowl.

Heat a grill pan over medium-low heat. Spread the sumac butter on each side of the bread slices and toast in the grill pan until golden brown on each side. Cut the toast into "soldiers."

Bring a pot of water to a rolling boil and prepare a bowl with lots of ice water. Slowly lower each egg into the water, taking care not to break them. Boil for exactly 6 minutes. Immediately remove the eggs from the boiling water and into the ice bath to shock them and stop the cooking. Leave them in the ice bath for 1 minute. Remove them and place them into egg cups.

Crack the tops off the eggs with a spoon and season the egg with salt and fresh black pepper. Dip the soldiers into the soft yolk.

PITA PIZZA

TOTALLY CUSTOMIZABLE

"What do you mean the pizza joint won't deliver at midnight?!" Apparently, things close down earlier when you leave the city of New York. I found this out drunkenly one night after moving down to Atlanta. Hence, the pita pizza.

MAKES 2 SERVINGS

INGREDIENTS

Tomato paste

2 pitas

Ancho Chili Harissa (page 215), optional

Grated kashkaval, provolone or mozzarella

Crumbled Bulgarian feta

Sliced green olives

Garlic, sliced finely

Olive oil

Fresh black pepper

METHOD

Preheat the broiler to high. Spread some tomato paste on the top of each pita. Add some harissa if you'd like it a bit spicy. Top with the grated *kashkaval*, crumbled feta cheese, sliced green olive and garlic. Drizzle with olive oil and season with fresh black pepper. Broil on high for 5–6 minutes until melty and toasty.

AVOCADO AND AMBA

PACKS A PUNCH!

Avocado toast has become something of a trend. I'm on it. My version is made with my favorite Middle Eastern condiment: *amba*. It's bright, intensely flavored and has the flavor of pickled fenugreek mangos. So tangy and powerful. You can find the recipe for amba on page 224 or just get the store-bought variety. Also, you can find anything on Amazon.

MAKES 1 SERVING

INGREDIENTS

Olive oil

2 thick slices pumpernickel

Salt and fresh black pepper

Amba (page 224)

½ avocado, sliced

Lemon

Maldon salt and fresh black pepper

METHOD

Heat a grill pan on high. Drizzle a generous amount of olive oil on each side of the slice of pumpernickel bread and season generously with salt and pepper. Grill each side for a minute or two until nicely charred and golden brown.

Spread a healthy amount of amba onto the toast, lay the slices of avocado on top, squeeze some lemon juice over top and season with just a bit of Maldon salt and fresh black pepper. Don't oversalt! The amba is already pickled! It's just to season the avocado.

CINNAMON CHALLAH

WITH SUGAR AND SALT

So you have a sweet tooth at night? You're like my husband. He also loves a good challah bread. This snack tastes like the love child of a cinnamon babka and a cinnamon bun.

MAKES 1 SERVING

INGREDIENTS

2 slices challah bread
4 tbsp (56 g) unsalted butter, softened
Brown sugar
Cinnamon
Maldon salt

METHOD

Preheat the broiler to high on your oven or toaster oven.

Spread the thick layer of softened butter on one side of the challah slices. Sprinkle with brown sugar and cinnamon.

Toast under the broiler for 3-4 minutes until the golden brown and smells intoxicating.

Sprinkle with Maldon salt.

BANANA NUTELLA PITA PANINI

NUTELLA. NUTELLA. BANANA. NUTELLA.

I literally have nothing to say to you other than Nutella. There is nothing like it on earth. There's a form of spreadable Israeli chocolate that was used in this classic afterschool snack in my childhood that works well, too. But it's no Nutella.

MAKES 1 SERVING

INGREDIENTS

1 pita
Nutella
½ banana, sliced
Maldon salt

METHOD

Slice the pita open so you have 2 round halves, like 2 slices of bread. Spread the Nutella on both insides of the pita halves and top 1 half with the bananas. Season with Maldon salt and place the other half on top to make a sandwich.

Heat a grill pan or panini press on medium-low heat. Grill, placing a heavy pan on top of the pita to press it down, for 2–3 minutes on each side until golden brown and warmed through.

SALADS AND SIDES

NO TABLE IS COMPLETE WITHOUT A MILLION SIDE DISHES

A lot of Israeli cuisine consists of mezes or tapas-style salads and sides that we call "*salatim*." I am proud to say that my family makes some bomb salatim. That's always our responsibility during holidays. "Can you bring all the salatim?" Which is probably the most labor-intensive job, since we make 8 to 12 different kinds. I've taken all of my family's recipes here and have turned them into great sides and salads that can hold their own. I've changed the techniques a bit, too. For example, instead of simply boiling, chopping and dressing the carrots to make Moroccan carrot salad, I've roasted the carrots whole in the spices and added a cooling yogurt sauce with a crunchy *dukkah*. That is a stand-alone side that I would even eat as a meal. These recipes will add a lot of those Israeli flavors to any meal you're making. So whether you're making just one as a side, or all of them for a nice "salatim" spread, people will be asking you for these recipes, just like friends ask for my family's recipes.

ULTIMATE ISRAELI SALAD

TEST YOUR KNIFE SKILLS

No breakfast, lunch or dinner is complete without a chopped Israeli salad. It's made slightly differently from place to place, but there is tomato and cucumber in it almost always. Chop this as finely and evenly as you can so you get a good combination of all the flavors in each bite.

MAKES 4 SERVINGS

INGREDIENTS

2 Roma tomatoes, diced finely

2 kirby cucumbers, diced finely

2 radishes, diced finely

½ yellow bell pepper, diced finely

½ red bell pepper, diced finely

¼ red onion, diced finely

1 ½ tbsp (2 g) chopped cilantro

1 ½ tbsp (2 g) chopped parsley

2 tbsp (30 ml) lemon juice

1 ½ tbsp (23 ml) olive oil

¼ tsp salt

METHOD

Combine the tomatoes, cucumbers, radishes, peppers, onion, cilantro and parsley in a big bowl. Dress with the lemon juice, olive oil and salt just before serving.

AYADA WITH QUICK-PICKLED BEETS

THE MOST GARLICKY MASHED POTATOES EVER

Ayada is a form of cold-whipped garlic mashed potatoes. You have to really like garlic to make the ayada. Like, really, really like garlic. I think the potatoes are just a carrier for the garlic and olive oil flavor. This is the most requested recipe that has come from my family's kitchen. I've added some lightly pickled beets to inject some fresh contrast. This can be eaten at room temperature or out of the fridge.

MAKES 6 SERVINGS

INGREDIENTS

3 small beets

2 tbsp (6 g) chopped parsley

2 tbsp (30 ml) lemon juice

1 tbsp (15 ml) olive oil

½ tsp white vinegar

½ tsp salt

2 pinches ground white pepper

3 medium white potatoes, peeled and cut in half

5–8 cloves garlic, minced

1 egg yolk

1 tsp salt

¼ cup (60 ml) olive oil

1 tbsp (15 ml) lemon juice

Olive oil

METHOD

Preheat the oven to 400°F (205°C). Wrap the beets in tinfoil. Roast in the oven for 30–40 minutes until fork tender. Depending on the size of the beets this may take a bit longer.

When the beets are cool enough to handle, rub the skin off of the beets with a paper towel. It should slip right off. Cut the beets into ½-inch (12-mm) pieces. Combine the beets with the parsley, lemon juice, olive oil, vinegar, salt and white pepper. Set in the fridge until you're ready to serve it.

Bring a large pot of water to a boil. Boil potatoes until they are fork tender. Reserve ¼ cup (60 ml) of the cooking liquid. Drain the potatoes. Push the potatoes through a ricer or mash them by hand.

In the bowl of a stand mixer with whisk attachment, whip the garlic, egg yolk and salt on medium speed until combined. Very slowly drizzle in half of the olive oil while the mixer is on to emulsify the mixture. Once the "aioli" is homogenized, add the mashed potatoes and continue to whip on medium speed. Slowly drizzle in the remaining olive oil and lemon juice. Slowly pour in the reserved cooking liquid from the potatoes. You'll need between 3 tablespoons (45 ml) to ¼ cup (60 ml) to get the potatoes to the desired consistency. Taste and adjust seasoning with salt and lemon juice accordingly.

Just before serving, plate the ayada and top with the beets. Drizzle with olive oil.

CARAMELIZED ONION & ALMOND RICE

DEEPLY FLAVORFUL & NUTTY

There are hundreds of rice recipes in the Middle East. Rice is a food group in and of itself. And you'll never find a plate of plain white rice. This was the plainest rice in my home: My mom would sauté onions before adding the rice to the pot and used consommé powder to flavor the cooking water. If you're going to eat rice, make it mean something. Have it complement the main dish. Don't let it be an afterthought. This rice goes well with, literally, anything. If there was any of this left over, I'd warm it up the next day and put a dollop of labane on top.

MAKES 4–6 SERVINGS

INGREDIENTS

1 ½ tbsp (23 ml) olive oil

1 large yellow onion, thinly sliced

1 cup (195 g) basmati or jasmine rice, rinsed

¼ cup (30 g) slivered almonds

2 cups (480 ml) chicken stock or water

1 tsp salt

½ tsp fresh black pepper

METHOD

Heat the oil in a saucepan over medium-low heat. Add the sliced onion and cook it down for 20 minutes until deep brown and caramelized, stirring often.

Stir in the rinsed rice and almonds and cook until the rice is slightly translucent and toasty, about 1 minute.

Turn the heat up to high, stir in the stock or water and season with the salt and pepper. Be sure to scrape the bottom and sides of the pot to ensure that the rice isn't stuck to it.

Bring to a boil, turn down the heat to low, cover and simmer for 20 minutes. Turn off the heat and let rest for 5 minutes before lifting the lid off.

Fluff and serve.

LENTIL & CHICKPEA SALAD

DRESSED WITH LEMON MUSTARD VINAIGRETTE

This salad is so hearty. I love making it to have it sit in the fridge for when I feel a bit snacky but want to keep carbs out of it. Make sure to keep the lentils al dente like a good French chef. The combination of dill, cilantro, mustard, lemon and lentils go so well together. It's herby and tangy with a bit of depth from the added cumin. This is a recipe I make over and over again. I've even been known to stuff it into a baguette.

MAKES 4–6 SERVINGS

INGREDIENTS

1 cup (200 g) green lentils

2 cups (480 ml) chicken or vegetable stock

½ tsp salt

¼ tsp fresh black pepper

1 bay leaf

1 (15 oz [425 g]) can chickpeas, drained and rinsed

¼ red onion, sliced ¼-inch (6-mm) thick

¼ cup (6 g) chopped dill

¼ cup (6 g) chopped cilantro

1 ½ tbsp (27 g) grainy mustard

1 ½ tbsp (23 ml) lemon juice

¼ cup (60 ml) olive oil

½ tsp salt

¼ tsp fresh black pepper

⅛ tsp cumin

METHOD

Bring the lentils, stock, salt, pepper and bay leaf to a boil in a saucepot over high heat. Cover, turn the heat down to low and simmer for 20–25 minutes until the lentils are al dente. Drain.

Combine the lentils with the chickpeas, red onion, dill and cilantro in a large bowl.

In a separate bowl, whisk together the mustard and lemon juice. Slowly stream in the olive oil while whisking to emulsify the dressing. Season with the salt, pepper and cumin and whisk to combine.

Pour the dressing over the lentils and chickpeas and toss to coat. Set in the fridge for 20 minutes to marinate and serve.

RAPINI TABBOULEH

BRIGHT, FRESH AND PACKED WITH PARSLEY

I've had to modify this recipe—traditionally made with just tomatoes, onions, parsley and couscous—a bit since my husband cringes at the thought of parsley. When making it for him, I double the rapini and leave the parsley out altogether. For this version, you get the best of both worlds using rapini *and* parsley. Instead of bulgur, you can use quinoa, farro or couscous. It can be made gluten-free, vegetarian, vegan . . . the whole nine yards. So make a big batch, take it in to work and don't forget a toothpick. You'll see why.

MAKES 6 SERVINGS

INGREDIENTS

¼ lb (110 g) rapini

1 ½ cups (290 g) cooked bulgur

1 Roma or vine-ripe tomato, diced finely

3 scallions, sliced finely

¼ cup (6 g) chopped parsley

2 tbsp (30 ml) freshly squeezed lemon juice

2 tsp (10 ml) olive oil

½ tsp salt

METHOD

Bring a large pot of salted water to a boil and prepare an ice bath.

Blanch the rapini for 2 ½ minutes then shock immediately in the ice bath. Drain and pat the rapini dry as much as possible.

Roughly chop the rapini and transfer to a large bowl. Add the bulgur, tomatoes, scallions, parsley, lemon juice, olive oil and salt and toss all together.

Store in the fridge for up to 2 days.

CARAWAY CABBAGE SLAW

DO YOU ENJOY RYE BREAD?

This is a really light slaw recipe. No mayo or heavy creams, just light and tangy. It works as a side, sandwich topper or a meze. The caraway seeds give the slaw a sort of rye bread flavor. Feel free to add shredded carrots or red cabbage. The only "don't" in this recipe is the substitution of black pepper for white pepper. It will throw the flavor off completely. White pepper is pickled when the berry is fully ripened. This gives it a tangy flavor note that black pepper does not have. Fast, easy, diet-friendly and tasty.

MAKES 6 SERVINGS

INGREDIENTS

¼ head white cabbage, finely shredded

2 ½ tbsp (38 ml) lemon juice

1 tbsp (15 ml) olive oil

1 tsp caraway seeds

¼ tsp salt

¼ tsp white pepper

METHOD

Combine all ingredients together and rest in the fridge for 30 minutes, mixing every 10 minutes. This will keep in the fridge for 1–2 days.

WATERCRESS & BEET SALAD

WITH LABANE DRESSING AND DUKKAH

You know those times when you look at the appetizers on a restaurant menu and you read "Beet and Goat Cheese Salad?" BORING. Come on. This would be a good alternative to that. It's excellently light, and the labane brings an element of creaminess to the dressing that goes a long way. Dress delicately!

MAKES 4 SERVINGS

INGREDIENTS

2 small beets
1 ½ tbsp (23 ml) olive oil
1 tbsp (15 g) Labane (page 219)
½ tbsp (8 ml) lemon juice
½ tbsp (8 ml) water
½ tsp Dijon mustard
Salt and fresh black pepper
1 bunch watercress
Dukkah (page 227)

METHOD

Preheat the oven to 400°F (205°C). Wrap the beets in tinfoil. Roast in the oven for 30–40 minutes until fork tender. Depending on the size of the beets, this may take a bit longer.

Make the dressing by whisking together the olive oil, labane, lemon juice, water, mustard, salt and fresh pepper to taste.

When the beets are cool enough to handle, rub the skin off the beets with a paper towel. It should slip right off. Cut the beets into ½-inch (12-mm) pieces. Season with a bit of salt.

Toss the watercress with just a tiny bit of dressing taking care not to drown the delicate leaves. Plate the watercress on the serving dish. Top the watercress with the beets, drizzle some dressing all over the dish and sprinkle with dukkah.

ROASTED RADISHES WITH SUMAC

AND BALSAMIC VINEGAR

Roasting softens the radishes' peppery flavor. They're beautiful vegetables. Probably the prettiest kind out there. The balsamic vinegar caramelizes and becomes sticky as it roasts with the radishes. Use whatever kind of radishes you can find at a farmer's market. If you are able to find black radishes, don't pass on them! They really are showstoppers.

MAKES 4–6 SERVINGS

INGREDIENTS

6 large or 12 small radishes, cut in half lengthwise

1 tbsp (15 ml) olive oil

Salt and fresh pepper

Balsamic vinegar

Sumac

Maldon salt

METHOD

Preheat the oven to 450°F (230°C) and lightly grease a baking sheet.

Toss the radishes with the olive oil and season with salt and fresh black pepper. Place them, cut side down, on the prepared baking sheet. Drizzle them with balsamic vinegar.

Roast in the oven for 15–18 minutes until cooked through and the cut side is slightly crisp.

Season with sumac and Maldon salt and serve warm or at room temperature.

SPICY HARISSA CARROTS

WITH WALNUTS

The combination of spicy and carrots is nothing new to Israeli and Middle Eastern cuisine. The sharp spice, tangy lemon juice and sweet honey penetrate the carrots to create a balance of flavors. Peeling the carrots into ribbons gives this dish more of a modern twist. Normally my mom would just cut them into half-inch slices . . . boring. Walnuts are added for texture. You can swap them out for pistachios too. Both work wonderfully.

MAKES 4 SERVINGS

INGREDIENTS

3 medium carrots

1 tbsp (15 ml) olive oil

2–3 cloves garlic, minced finely

1 ½ tbsp (6 g) Ancho Chili Harissa (page 215)

¼ cup (45 g) walnuts, chopped

1 tsp honey

1 ½ tbsp (23 ml) lemon juice

2 tsp (1 g) chopped parsley

½ tsp salt

METHOD

Using a vegetable peeler, peel and discard the outer layer of the carrots. Continue to peel around the core of the carrots to form ribbons into a large bowl. Discard the cores of the carrots.

Heat a small pan over medium-low. Add the olive oil, garlic, harissa, walnuts and honey. Warm through until fragrant, about 2 minutes. Immediately pour over the carrot ribbons.

Add the lemon juice, parsley and salt and toss to combine. Let marinate for at least 30 minutes before serving, the longer the better. This will keep in the fridge for up to 1 day.

DILL AND MINT MASH

HERBY

Can't write a cookbook without throwing in a potato mash recipe! This one is super dilly and minty. It goes really well with any fish or chicken dish. You can even top it with some *kofta* kebabs. Super versatile and delightful.

MAKES 4 SERVINGS

INGREDIENTS

3 medium white potatoes, peeled and cut in half

2 tbsp (30 ml) olive oil

2 tbsp (30 ml) heavy cream (35%–40%)

1 clove garlic, minced

1 ½ tbsp (2 g) chopped mint

1 ½ tbsp (2 g) chopped dill

1 tsp salt

METHOD

Bring a large pot of water to a boil. Boil potatoes until they are fork tender. Reserve 2 tablespoons (30 ml) of the cooking liquid. Drain the potatoes. Push the potatoes through a ricer or mash them by hand.

Combine the potatoes with the olive oil, heavy cream, garlic, mint, dill, salt and the reserved cooking liquid. Serve warm or at room temperature.

FRESH CUCUMBER, FENNEL & RADISH SALAD

WITH SUMAC. ALWAYS WITH SUMAC.

The combination of radish, cucumber and fennel feels right for an outdoor picnic or BBQ. It's got the right crunch and the right amount of acidity that melds the flavors together. And sumac makes it pretty. Duh.

MAKES 4 SERVINGS

INGREDIENTS

2 kirby cucumbers, sliced ¼-inch (6-mm) thick

½ fennel bulb, sliced ⅛-inch (3-mm) thick

2 radishes, sliced ⅛-inch (3-mm) thick

1 tbsp (1.5 g) chopped dill

1 tbsp (15 ml) lemon juice

½ tbsp (8 ml) olive oil

Sumac

Salt

METHOD

Toss the cucumbers, fennel, radishes, dill, lemon juice and olive oil together in a bowl, seasoning with sumac and salt to taste.

ROASTED JERUSALEM ARTICHOKES

WITH ROSEMARY AND BALSAMIC VINEGAR

They taste like an artichoke but have the texture of a potato. They're also called sunchokes. It's so confusing, and I love it. Weird and knobby, but absolutely tasty. Here, I roast them on a bed of rosemary sprigs. It will fill your home with a warming scent and feeling. Try this recipe out next time you need to make some sort of roasted vegetable as a side.

MAKES 4 SERVINGS

INGREDIENTS

Rosemary sprigs

½ lb (225 g) Jerusalem artichokes, scrubbed and cut into 1-inch (2.5-cm) pieces

2 tbsp (30 ml) olive oil

Salt and fresh black pepper

2 tbsp (30 ml) balsamic vinegar

METHOD

Preheat the oven to 375°F (190°C) and lightly grease a baking sheet and line the whole sheet with rosemary sprigs.

Toss the artichokes with the olive oil and season with salt and pepper. Place them on top of the rosemary sprigs on the baking sheet and drizzle with the balsamic vinegar.

Roast in the oven for 45–50 minutes, turning the artichokes twice during the roasting process. Let cool at least 5 minutes before serving. Use the rosemary as a garnish.

SWEETS

AND THEN THERE WAS SUGAR.

Desserts were never my thing. I always enjoyed eating them, though. Pastry came a lot later in my culinary career, and I'm so happy it did. These recipes are a combination of dishes I've dreamt up and others that are more nostalgic. Pardon me if I get a little sentimental during this chapter. Like the chocolate-covered cornflakes. My mom would make that dessert for us after every accomplishment in our lives, and occasionally as a "just because I love you" treat. Others, like the halva morning buns, are recipes that I've flexed my creative writing biceps. You will find that I garnish a lot of my desserts with salt. Well, that's because I'm a chef, and also because it's freaking delicious.

LABANE PANNA COTTA

WITH POMEGRANATE JELLY

After a Middle Eastern meal, you'd be served something called *malabi* for dessert. It's a custard flavored with rosewater. It can be made dairy free. Ew. But some people really love it. I, for one, freaking love dairy and don't love rosewater. This dessert looks like a malabi, but tastes so much better. I've made this into a panna cotta using labane as the main dairy ingredient. I give you the option of using rosewater instead of the vanilla bean paste. They both work really nicely in the panna cotta. Be creative and use a different fruit for the jelly! Mangos would be on point here.

MAKES 4 SERVINGS

INGREDIENTS

1 cup (240 ml) pomegranate juice

1 ½ tsp (6 g) gelatin powder

2 tbsp (30 ml) water

1 ½ tsp (6 g) gelatin powder

1 cup (125 g) Labane (page 219)

1 tsp vanilla bean paste or rosewater

½ cup (120 ml) heavy whipping cream (35%–40%)

½ cup (120 ml) milk

¼ cup (50 g) sugar

Pomegranate seeds

Chopped pistachios

METHOD

Combine 2 tablespoons (30 ml) of the pomegranate juice with the gelatin powder in a measuring cup with a spout for easy pouring. Let the gelatin bloom for 10 minutes, untouched.

Heat the remaining pomegranate juice over medium-low heat until it just comes to a simmer. Add the warmed pomegranate juice to the measuring cup with the bloomed gelatin and mix to dissolve. Pour equally into 4 serving glasses. Set them in the fridge to set for at least 1 hour.

Combine the gelatin with the water and let bloom for 10 minutes. In a large mixing bowl, combine the labane and the vanilla bean paste or rosewater.

Heat the cream, milk and sugar over medium heat until the mixture is just about to bubble around the edges and the sugar has dissolved. Add the bloomed gelatin and mix to dissolve. Pour the milk and gelatin mixture into the bowl with the labane and mix to combine. Pour the mixture into the measuring cup with the spout for easy pouring.

Pour equal amounts into the serving glasses, slowly, not to disturb the already set pomegranate jelly. Set back in the fridge to set for at least 3 hours.

Top with pomegranate seeds and chopped pistachios and serve.

SALTED TAHINI CHOCOLATE CHIP COOKIES

OH. GOD.

I own a cookie shop in Toronto. There needed to be a cookie recipe in this book. I dream that one day we will sell these in the shop. Luckily for me, the world has warmed to the idea of using tahini in desserts. I use it a lot. These are super soft in the middle and crispy on the edges, just like a perfect cookie should be. Use the best-quality chocolate you can find. I use Valrhona discs here because their shape and taste are superior to any chocolate I've tested with this recipe.

MAKES 12 COOKIES

INGREDIENTS

8 tbsp (113 g) room temperature unsalted butter

½ cup (120 ml) sesame paste

1 cup (225 g) sugar

1 large egg

1 egg yolk

1 tsp vanilla extract

1 cup plus 2 tbsp (150 g) all-purpose flour

½ tsp baking soda

½ tsp baking powder

1 tsp salt

1 ¾ cup (230 g) Valrhona discs (64% cocoa)

Maldon salt

METHOD

In the bowl of an electric mixer fitted with paddle attachment, cream the butter, sesame paste and sugar together on medium speed until light in color and fluffy, about 5 minutes.

Add the egg, egg yolk and vanilla extract and continue mixing on medium speed for another 5 minutes.

Sift the flour, baking soda, baking powder and salt into a large bowl and combine. Add the flour mixture to the butter mixture and mix on low until just combined.

Add the chocolate discs and mix them in by hand with a rubber spatula.

Line a baking sheet with parchment paper. Using a 2-ounce (60-ml)-capacity ice-cream disher (scoop with release), scoop out 12 dough balls and place them on the baking sheet. Wrap the baking sheet with plastic wrap and place it in the freezer for no less than 12 hours. This will allow the glutens in the flour to relax and will give you a tender soft cookie. Do not skip this step.

At this point you can bake 1 or bake all 12. Keep the cookie dough balls in zip-top bags in the freezer for up to 6 months.

Preheat the oven to 325°F (160°C) and line a baking sheet with parchment or silicone mat. Space the cookie-dough balls at least 3 inches (7.5 cm) apart to allow for them to spread. Bake for 13–16 minutes until just golden brown around the edges. They will still look fairly unbaked in the middle, which is perfect. Sprinkle each with Maldon salt when they come out of the oven.

Allow to cool for 20 minutes on baking sheet or cooling rack.

ADULT "MILKY"

POTS DE CREME

Milky is the Israeli form of a chocolate Jell-O pudding. It's a chocolate pudding with a whipped cream on top. Everyone who has grown up in Israel or in an Israeli home has had these in their lifetime. Heck, I still have them when I can find them in the grocery store. This is my refined, adultified version of a Milky. Leave out the coffee and the liquor if you're serving to children . . . or don't. I won't judge.

MAKES 6 SHAREABLE SERVINGS

INGREDIENTS

1 ⅓ cups (175 g) good-quality semisweet chocolate

2 ½ cups (600 ml) heavy whipping cream (35%–40%)

1 tsp vanilla extract

1 tsp instant espresso powder

2 tbsp (30 ml) good quality whiskey

5 egg yolks, room temperature

3 tbsp (15 g) sugar

½ tsp salt

1 ½ cups (360 ml) heavy whipping cream (35%–40%)

3 tbsp (15 g) sugar

½ tsp vanilla extract

Dark chocolate, for garnish

METHOD

Place the chocolate in a large heatproof bowl.

Heat the cream, vanilla, espresso powder and whiskey over medium heat until it just starts to come to a simmer. Immediately pour the mixture over the chocolate and let it sit for 4 minutes until the chocolate has melted. Whisk to combine. Let this cool for 15 minutes.

In a separate large mixing bowl, whisk together the egg yolks, sugar and salt until the mixture is lighter in color and ribbony. This will take at least 2 minutes of whisking.

Slowly pour the chocolate mixture into the egg yolk mixture while whisking to combine. Continue mixing until you have a homogenous chocolate mix. Let this come to room temperature.

Preheat the oven to 325°F (160°C). Place 6 mason jars (½ pint [235 ml]) into a large baking pan, leaving at least 1 inch (2.5 cm) of room between them. Pour the chocolate mixture equally among the mason jars. Pour enough hot water into the baking pan to come halfway up the mason jars. Cover the baking pan, tightly, with tinfoil. Pierce a few holes in the tinfoil. This will allow the steam to escape in the oven.

Carefully transfer the baking pan into the oven and bake for 35 minutes. The custard should still be slightly jiggly. Remove the mason jars from the baking pan and allow to cool to room temperature. Transfer them to the fridge and allow to set for about 4 hours.

To make the whipped cream, whisk together the heavy cream, sugar and vanilla extract in a cold metal bowl until stiff peaks form. This can be done in an electric mixer, too.

Before serving, evenly disperse the whipped cream among the mason jars, topping the chocolate custard. Shave a bit of dark chocolate over top. Serve.

EVERYTHING FRUIT SALAD

OVER KADAIF NESTS

Time to venture outside of the ordinary. This fruit salad has a lot of different kinds of fruit and berries, but you will not see a banana, apple or basic pear. Grab the freshest fruit. The only important fruit here is the lychee and its juice. Funny enough, it's the only fruit I use that isn't actually fresh. Cheat: Hit up the grocery store precut fruit containers you find in the produce section if you don't want to buy a whole melon or pineapple. *Kadaif* can be found in the frozen section near the puff pastry. It's basically a shredded phyllo dough. It's super fun to eat and literally gets everywhere.

MAKES 4 SHAREABLE SERVINGS

INGREDIENTS

20 oz (565 g) canned lychee in juice

¼ cantaloupe, cut into ¼-inch (6-mm) cubes

¼ honeydew melon, cut into ¼-inch (6-mm) cubes

¼ pineapple, cut into ¼-inch (6-mm) cubes

¼ prickly pear, cut into ¼-inch (6-mm) cubes

1 kiwi, cut into ¼-inch (6-mm) cubes

6 strawberries, sliced into quarters

6 blackberries, sliced into quarters

8 raspberries, sliced into quarters

10–12 red grapes, sliced into quarters

⅛ cup (20 g) pomegranate seeds

½ package frozen *kadaif*, thawed in the fridge

8 tbsp (113 g) melted unsalted butter

½ tsp cornstarch

2 tsp (10 ml) water

Star fruit, sliced ¼-inch (6-mm) thick

METHOD

Drain the lychee and reserve the juice from the can. Pit and cut the lychee into ¼-inch (6-mm) pieces.

Combine the lychee, cantaloupe, honeydew, pineapple, prickly pear, kiwi, strawberries, blackberries, raspberries, grapes and pomegranate seeds in a large bowl and toss to combine. Pour in the reserved lychee juice, cover and let the flavors marinate in the fridge for 1 hour.

Preheat the oven to 375°F (190°C) and line a baking sheet with parchment paper. In a large bowl, combine the *kadaif* and butter. Make four equal 6-inch- (15-cm) diameter nests on the baking sheet, making sure there is a decent-size well in the middle for the fruit salad to sit in.

Bake for 10–12 minutes until golden brown.

To make the juice syrup, strain the fruit salad liquid into a saucepan. Reduce the sauce over medium-high heat until there is about ½ cup (120 ml) left. This will concentrate the flavors. In a small bowl, dissolve the cornstarch in the water. Add this mixture to the simmering juice syrup and allow to bubble for another minute until thickened.

Place the kadaif nest onto the serving dishes, top with a generous amount of fruit salad onto the nests and drizzle the fruit and plate with the juice syrup. Garnish with sliced star fruit and serve.

BUTTERED RUM BANANAS

WITH SWEET TAHINI SAUCE OVER ICE CREAM

Tahini paste isn't just used for savory dishes, it can be sweetened like any nut butter. When we had company over, my dad would serve ice cream drizzled with tahini paste and date molasses and then top it with halva. It made for a very impressive dessert. I know it sounds strange, but trust me on this. It's very tasty. Here, tahini paste is sweetened with honey, drizzled over ice cream and then topped with buttery sautéed bananas and Maldon salt to finish. Don't you dare skip the salt. The tahini sauce can be made ahead of time, but I recommend making the bananas on the spot. It. Is. Mind-blowing. Add some crumbled pretzels for added crunch!

MAKES 4 SERVINGS

INGREDIENTS

⅓ cup (80 ml) sesame paste

3 tbsp (45 ml) water

2 ½ tbsp (38 ml) honey

Pinch salt

4 tbsp (56 g) unsalted butter

2 bananas, sliced diagonally ½-inch (12-mm) thick

1 tbsp (15 g) granulated sugar

1 ½ tbsp (23 ml) good-quality light rum

Good-quality vanilla bean ice cream

Maldon salt

Black sesame seeds

METHOD

For the tahini sauce, whisk together the sesame paste, water and honey with a pinch of salt. Keep whisking until the mixture is homogenous.

Heat the butter in a large frying pan over medium heat. As soon as the butter has melted, add the bananas to the pan in one layer. Sprinkle the sugar over the sliced bananas. Let cook for 1–2 minutes until slightly browned around the edges. Flip the bananas and cook for another minute.

Pour in the rum, and if you have the *cojones* plus *the proper ventilation system* in your kitchen, flame the bananas. This step is optional. Let the alcohol cook off for about 30 seconds. Swirl the bananas around in the pan. Cook for another minute then take the pan off the heat.

Portion out 2 small scoops of ice cream into each serving dish. Drizzle the tahini sauce over the ice cream and top with the bananas. Garnish with Maldon salt and black sesame seeds. Serve any extra tahini sauce on the side.

WHIPPED CHEESECAKE

WITH PECAN COOKIE CRUST AND CRUMBLE

This is the perfect finish to a family meal. Our family has one, and only one, person who will always make this dessert. No one else has it in them to even give it a shot. I've changed it so that it's more of an American-Israeli cross between a crumble cheesecake and a whipped-cream kind of dessert. I've also added pecans because I like the texture it adds to the crumble. This is a great dessert to bring to the next dinner party you're invited to. Super easy and can be made ahead!

MAKES 8–10 SERVINGS

INGREDIENTS

14 tbsp (200 g) room-temperature unsalted butter

⅓ cup (75 g) dark-brown sugar

2 egg yolks

1 tsp vanilla extract

2 cups (250 g) self-rising flour

¼ tsp salt

⅓ cup (55 g) chopped pecans

1 cup (240 ml) heavy whipping cream (35%–40%)

½ cup (100 g) sugar

1 cup (250 g) Labane (page 219) or sour cream

1 cup (250 g) mascarpone

1 ½ tsp (8 ml) vanilla-bean paste

¼ tsp salt

METHOD

Preheat the oven to 325°F (165°C).

In the bowl of an electric mixer fitted with paddle attachment, cream the butter and sugar until light and fluffy. Add the yolks and vanilla and continue creaming for another 3 minutes. Add in the flour and salt and mix on low until the dough comes together.

Transfer ½ of the dough into an 8-inch x 11-inch (20-cm x 28-cm) baking dish and press it evenly along the bottom.

Add the pecans to the remaining dough and mix to combine. Transfer the pecan dough to a separate 8-inch x 11-inch (20-cm x 28-cm) baking dish and press it evenly along the bottom. This will be your crumb topping, so you can use a different-size baking dish, but keep it similar in size.

Bake for 12–15 minutes until golden brown. Cool to room temperature.

In a bowl of an electric mixer with whisk attachment, whip the heavy cream and sugar until stiff peaks form. Add the labane, mascarpone, vanilla-bean paste and salt. Whip on medium speed to combine until light and airy, 3–4 minutes.

Spread the cheesecake mixture onto the plain cookie crust in an even layer. Using your hands, crumble the pecan cookie sheet evenly over the cheesecake.

Cover and chill in the fridge for at least 1 hour.

TAHINI-SWIRLED BROWNIES

FUDGY AND NUTTY

I've loved peanut-butter brownies all my life. There was this one bake shop near my place in the East Village that would make super-fudgy ones, and on my way home from work every Friday, I would pick one up and savor it on my walk. This has been a secret of mine until this moment. A brownie a week does the body and mind some good. So, I thought, *Why not a brownie with sesame paste?* I couldn't find one reason not to make it happen.

MAKES 16 BROWNIES

INGREDIENTS

1 cup (125 g) all-purpose flour

2 tbsp (20 g) unsweetened cocoa powder

1 tsp salt

10 tbsp (142 g) unsalted butter

7 oz (200 g) good quality semi-sweet chocolate, roughly chopped

½ cup (110 g) brown sugar

1 cup (200 g) sugar

3 large eggs

1 ½ tsp (8 ml) vanilla extract

¼ cup (60 ml) sesame paste

METHOD

Preheat the oven to 325°F (165°C). Prepare a 9-inch x 12-inch (23-cm x 30-cm) baking pan by lining it with parchment paper leaving an overhang on two sides for easy brownie removal. Lightly grease any exposed sides of the pan with cooking spray.

Sift and combine the flour, cocoa and salt in a mixing bowl. Set aside.

In a double broiler, melt the butter and chocolate in a heatproof bowl. As soon as the butter and chocolate has completely melted, take the bowl off the heat and stir in the brown sugar and sugar until just combined. Add in the eggs and vanilla extract and mix until the mixture is homogenous. Add in the flour mixture and fold it into the chocolate mixture carefully. Once the batter is just mixed and there are no lumps of flour, pour it into the prepared baking pan.

Dollop the sesame paste onto the brownie batter in different spots and swirl using a knife or skewer. Bake for 20–23 minutes until the brownie is set. Let this cool to room temperature before cutting into it.

Cut into 3-inch x 4-inch (7.5-cm x 10-cm) rectangles.

ROASTED BANANA CHOCOLATE POPS

ICE CREAM POPS

You're on the beach, it's hot and all you want is an ice cream, but you are too lazy to get up. Then you hear: "ICE CREAM, ICE POPS, STRAWBERRY, LEMON, BANANA CHOCOLATE!" Someone has answered your prayers. The sweaty, super-tanned, 50-year-old skinny man has just walked by you with his huge Styrofoam ice-cream-filled cooler he's got on his shoulder. You get a hold of him and magically, you're enjoying your hot-yellow-colored banana ice cream pop covered in a hard chocolate shell.

MAKES 12 POPS

INGREDIENTS

4 ripe bananas, sliced ½-inch (12-mm) thick

¼ cup (50 g) sugar

½ tsp salt

3 tbsp (42 g) unsalted butter, cut into ¼-inch (6-mm) pieces

⅓ cup (80 ml) heavy whipping cream (35%–40%)

1 ½ cups (360 ml) milk

1 tsp vanilla extract

4 oz (113 g) good-quality dark chocolate, chopped roughly

METHOD

Preheat the oven to 375°F (190°C).

In a mixing bowl, toss the bananas with the sugar and salt. Transfer them to a baking dish and dot the bananas with the pieces of butter.

Roast for 35–40 minutes until the bananas are golden brown and caramelized. Depending on the ripeness of the bananas and your oven, this may take more or less time, so please keep an eye on the browning. Let cool to room temperature.

Transfer the roasted bananas with any accumulated juice into a blender. Add in the cream, milk and vanilla. Blend on high until smooth.

Pour the mixture into ice pop molds, cover and add popsicle sticks to the mold. Freeze for at least 6 hours.

Melt the chocolate over a double boiler until smooth. Remove the popsicles from the molds and drizzle with the melted chocolate.

These can be stored in the freezer in an airtight container with parchment between the pops.

HONEY & APPLE CAKE

WITH WALNUT CARAMEL SAUCE

This cake is big. It's super tall and dripping beautifully with walnut caramel. For Rosh Hashanah, Jews eat slices of apples dipped in honey in hopes of a sweet new year. This cake is definitely sweet and is packed with apples. Don't be afraid of a little color on the outside of the cake as it bakes. It adds a great taste and somewhat of a crust for the soft inside.

MAKES 9-INCH (23-CM) CAKE

INGREDIENTS

3 cups (400 g) all-purpose flour

2 tsp (16 g) baking soda

1 tsp salt

1 tsp cinnamon

1 cup (240 ml) buttermilk

⅔ cup (160 ml) honey

1 tbsp (15 ml) blackstrap molasses

8 tbsp (113 g) room temperature unsalted butter

½ cup (120 ml) canola oil

⅔ cup (150 g) brown sugar

2 eggs

3 large honey crisp apples, peeled and cut into ¼-inch (6-mm) pieces

5 tbsp (70 g) unsalted butter

¾ cup (165 g) brown sugar

⅓ cup (80 ml) heavy whipping cream (35%–40%)

1 cup (100 g) walnuts

½ tsp salt

METHOD

Preheat the oven to 325°F (165°C). Grease a 9-inch (23-cm) springform pan and line the bottom with a 9-inch (23-cm) round parchment sheet.

Sift the flour, baking soda, salt and cinnamon into a mixing bowl and mix to combine. In a separate bowl, mix the buttermilk, honey and molasses. Set aside.

In the bowl of an electric mixer with paddle attachment, cream the butter, oil and sugar together on medium speed until combined. Add the eggs and mix until combined, lighter in color and fluffy. Add in half of the flour mixture and mix on low until just combined. Pour in the buttermilk mixture and mix on low until just combined. Add in the remaining flour mixture and combine until smooth and homogenous.

Fold in the apples by hand with a rubber spatula. Pour the batter into the pan, set the pan onto a baking sheet and bake in the middle of the oven for 45–50 minutes until cooked through, checking with wooden skewer that the cake is no longer wet inside. Set aside to cool completely.

For the caramel sauce, heat the butter, sugar and cream in a heavy-bottom saucepan over medium-low heat. Cook and whisk constantly until the sauce has thickened. Turn the heat off, add in the walnuts and salt and mix to combine.

Remove the cake from the springform pan and set on a plate or cake stand. Pour the walnut caramel over top.

HALVA MORNING BUNS

WITH WHITE CHOCOLATE

Buns are the best. Especially the inner parts that stay super soft. These morning buns are made with an easy yeast dough and are filled with halva and white chocolate. Israeli halva is a sweetened sesame confection. You can walk through the market in Jerusalem and get slices of it with all kinds of flavors and mix-ins. For this recipe, I recommend a basic plain or vanilla-flavored halva. So. Good.

MAKES 8 BUNS

INGREDIENTS

⅓ cup (80 ml) milk

8 tbsp (113 g) unsalted butter

2 ¼ tsp (8 g) dry active yeast, one packet

3 cups (375 g) all-purpose flour

¼ cup (30 g) almond flour

⅓ cup (70 g) brown sugar

1 tsp salt

½ tsp cinnamon

2 large eggs

1 ½ tsp (23 ml) vanilla extract

1 ½ cups (260 g) plain halva

1 cup (175 g) white chocolate chips

METHOD

Warm the milk and the butter in a saucepan over medium heat until the butter has melted. Transfer the milk mixture to a bowl. Let it cool slightly. The milk shouldn't be warmer than 115°F (46°C) or else it will kill the yeast. Add in the yeast and let it sit for 10 minutes until the yeast is foamy.

Combine the flour, almond flour, sugar, salt and cinnamon in the bowl of an electric mixer with dough-hook attachment. Add the eggs and vanilla extract to the milk and yeast mixture and whisk to combine. Pour the wet ingredients into the dry ingredients and mix on low until just combined, about 2 minutes. Turn the dough out onto a lightly floured surface and knead for 2–3 minutes. The dough should be sticky.

Transfer the dough into a lightly greased bowl, cover and set it in a warm place to rise for at least 1 hour.

Grease a muffin tin with melted butter. Roll the dough out on a lightly floured surface to a 16-inch x 12-inch (40-cm x 30-cm) rectangle. Crumble the halva all over the surface of the dough and roll over it with the pin so it's pressed into the dough. Scatter the white chocolate chips all over the dough. Roll the dough as tightly as possible along the longer edge to get a 16-inch (40-cm) long sausage roll. Cut the roll into 8 large pieces.

Transfer all the pieces into the muffin tins with the cut side up. Cover with a kitchen towel and place in a warm place to rise again for another hour.

Preheat the oven to 350°F (175°C). Place the buns in the oven and bake for 25 minutes until golden brown and baked through.

FROZEN CHOCOLATE CORNFLAKE BARS

CRUNCHY TREAT

I don't know where this recipe came from, but I remember loving it growing up. It had been years since I made it. I ate the whole thing in a few days, all by myself. I tried to erase it from my mind, but I couldn't erase it from the scale as easily, unfortunately. This is a frozen, crunchy, chocolaty treat. It needs to be kept frozen because of the butter content in there. But the incredible part is that it begins to melt immediately in your mouth. Use Israeli semisweet chocolate if you can find it!

MAKES 9 BARS

INGREDIENTS

6 oz (170 g) good-quality semisweet chocolate, chopped roughly

12 tbsp (170 g) unsalted butter, cut into large pieces

4 cups (115 g) plain cornflakes (not frosted)

Maldon salt

METHOD

Prepare a 9-inch x 6-inch (23-cm x 15 cm) baking pan by lining it with parchment and leaving an overhang on two sides for easy removal.

In a double broiler, melt the chocolate and butter until smooth. Mix the chocolate mixture with the cornflakes in a large bowl. Once the cornflakes are completely coated with chocolate, pour into the prepared baking sheet and press down into an even layer. Sprinkle with Maldon salt.

Place it in the freezer for at least 1 hour until frozen through. Cut into 3-inch x 2-inch (7.5-cm x 5-cm) bars. Store in an airtight container in the freezer with parchment paper between them.

POMEGRANATE GRANITA

TANGY AND REFRESHING

Easily the most refreshing dessert to any meal. Even if you are stuffed to the brim, you can't say no to a granita. This one is tangy because of the pomegranate molasses and super light. It cleanses the palate beautifully.

MAKES 6 SERVINGS

INGREDIENTS

1 ½ cups (360 ml) pomegranate juice
2 ½ tbsp (38 ml) pomegranate molasses
Chopped mint
Pomegranate seeds

METHOD

Combine the juice and molasses together and pour into a baking dish. Carefully place it in the freezer. Allow to freeze for at least 3 hours, making sure to scrape it with a fork once an hour.

Serve with chopped mint and pomegranate seeds.

STAPLES

BASIC SAUCES AND CONCOCTIONS

These are items that an Israeli will always have in their fridge or can whip up right away. I have to admit that I've bought a lot of these items because I don't always have the patience to make them. These recipes are here for you if you can't find an item in the grocery store or if you just feel like being super culinary. FYI: Fermentation and pickling are so in right now.

TAHINI

LIQUID GOLD

We put this sh*t on everything. Falafel, shawarma, steak, schnitzel. . . . We bake meatballs in it. We even put it on hummus. Sauce on sauce. It's like what ketchup is to America, but white.

MAKES ABOUT 1 ½ CUPS (360 ML)

INGREDIENTS

⅔ cup (160 ml) sesame paste
½ cup (120 ml) water
3 cloves garlic, finely minced
2 tbsp (30 ml) fresh lemon juice
1 tbsp (1.5 g) chopped parsley
½ tsp salt

METHOD

Whisk all of the ingredients together. Keep on whisking, it will come together. It should be runny. If you find that it is too thick, add a bit more water. Adjust seasoning to taste with salt and lemon juice.

ANCHO CHILI HARISSA

GIVE THE MIDDLE EAST A MEXICAN FLAIR

Harissa is made everywhere in the Middle East. The recipe varies. I love the flavor the dried ancho chilies give to this one, although ancho is not normally a pepper you would find in a regular harissa. It should be deeply red in color and fairly thick. More like a spread than a hot sauce. I've been known to whisk it into some eggs to create a fire red frittata. Mix it into ketchup or mayo for added kick to basic condiments. It's perfectly spicy.

MAKES ABOUT 1 CUP (250 G)

INGREDIENTS

6 dried ancho chili peppers

6 dried guajillo peppers

2 Thai bird's-eye chilis, or more for spicier harissa, stems removed

4 cloves garlic

2 tbsp (30 ml) olive oil

2 tsp (10 ml) lemon juice

1 tsp hot paprika

¼ tsp coriander

¼ tsp cumin

¼ tsp caraway seeds

1 ¼ tsp (7 g) salt

METHOD

Place the dried peppers in a bowl and cover them with boiling water. Let steep for 15 minutes until the peppers are soft. Drain the water.

Cut off the stems and transfer the peppers to a food processor along with the Thai chilis and garlic. Pulse until smooth. Make sure to push down any large pieces stuck to the side of the processor.

Add the olive oil, lemon juice, paprika, coriander, cumin, caraway seeds and salt. Process until smooth.

Store in an airtight container in the fridge for up to 4 weeks.

MILD RED PEPPER HARISSA

NOT SO HAWT SAUCE

I like hot sauce. Not the hurts-your-mouth, painful hot sauce. The kind that actually tastes good and adds flavor to a dish. This is a roasted-red-pepper-flavored harissa. It's definitely milder than your usual harissa. If you like the flavor, but you have a death wish/enjoy S&M, add more of the Thai chilis and a bit more hot paprika.

MAKES ABOUT 1 CUP (200 G)

INGREDIENTS

1 large yellow onion, roughly chopped

12 cloves garlic, crushed

1 Thai bird's-eye chili, optional, do not use for mild version

3 tbsp (45 ml) olive oil

2 large roasted red peppers, jarred is fine, roughly chopped

3 tbsp (45 ml) olive oil

1 ½ tbsp (23 ml) fresh lemon juice

2 tsp (9 g) tomato paste

1 tsp caraway seeds

½ tsp hot paprika

½ tsp salt

½ tsp ground coriander

¼ tsp cumin

METHOD

Heat 3 tablespoons (45 ml) of olive oil in a large frying pan over medium-high heat. Add the onion, garlic and chilis to the pan and fry for 6–8 minutes, tossing occasionally, until nicely charred. Set aside to cool.

Transfer the mixture from the pan to a food processor. Add the remaining ingredients and blitz until smooth. If the harissa is too thick, add an additional tablespoon or two (15–30 ml) of olive oil.

Store in an airtight container in the fridge for up to 3 weeks.

LABANE

MY FAVORITE INGREDIENT EVER

It's smooth, creamy, salty and, not to mention, lower in fat than any cream cheese or spreadable cheese you will find. Every time I put it out when we have friends over, someone always asks, "Ooooooh, what is this?" I use it a lot throughout my recipes, so if you can't seem to find it in the grocery store, this is a really easy way to make it. It should be thick and spreadable. Normally this spread is served simply on a plate with olive oil and za'atar. You can feel free to mix in chopped green olives for added texture and flavor. I do that often.

MAKES ABOUT 2 CUPS (500 G)

INGREDIENTS

1 lb (454 g) plain yogurt
1 tsp kosher salt

METHOD

Place a strainer over a large bowl and line it with 4 layers of cheesecloth. Mix the yogurt and salt together and pour onto the cheesecloth. Allow to drain in the fridge for at least 8 hours or longer.

It will keep in an airtight container in the fridge for up to 3 days.

Plate the labane, drizzle with olive oil and season with za'atar. Alternatively, mix with chopped green olives.

SCHUG

SUPER GREEN

This is a different kind of Middle Eastern hot sauce. It's green and herby. You can adjust the spice level by the number of hot peppers you put in. I make a big batch and freeze it in smaller containers. It's great as a topping or even as a flavoring agent. Stir some into a tortilla soup. So good.

MAKES ABOUT 1 ½ CUPS (150 G)

INGREDIENTS

1 whole bunch cilantro
1 whole bunch parsley
2 hot long peppers, stems removed
2 jalapeño peppers, stems removed
½ cup (120 ml) water
8 cloves garlic
½ tsp salt
¼ tsp cumin

METHOD

Place all the ingredients into a food processor and blitz until finely chopped.

This will keep in the fridge in an airtight container for 5 days or in the freezer for 3 months.

PRESERVED LEMONS

WITH MUSTARD SEEDS

Sour and pungent, preserved lemons are used throughout Middle Eastern cuisines. They're pickled in their own juice, which is kind of messed up if you think about it. The peel becomes soft and edible. I really love their distinct flavor. Try adding some chopped preserved lemons to a salsa or salad dressing for a nice spin on a classic.

MAKES 5 LEMONS

INGREDIENTS

6–8 lemons
⅔ cup (210 g) kosher salt
2 tbsp (30 g) sugar
¼ tsp turmeric
½ cup (120 ml) lemon juice
½ tsp yellow mustard seeds

METHOD

Prepare and sanitize a 1-quart (475-ml) mason jar and lid.

Cut the lemons by quartering them and leaving at least ¼-inch (6-mm) from the bottom of the lemon uncut so that the whole lemon still holds together.

In a large bowl, combine the salt, sugar and turmeric. Drop the lemons into the bowl and shove the salt mixture into the center of the lemons to pack them. Push as many lemons as you can fit into the jar. Really squish them in there.

Pour the salt mixture onto the lemons along with the lemon juice and mustard seeds. If the lemons are not completely submerged, top up with water until they are.

Seal and set to pickle in a spot where they will sit in some sunlight. They will need at least a month to pickle through. Once in a while give them a bit of a shake.

Once you open the jar, they will keep for up to 5 months. Rinsing the lemons before using is optional depending on how salty/intense you need them to be.

AMBA

MANGO CHUTNEY CONDIMENT

My dad would get home from work and be starving. He would walk straight into the kitchen, unable to wait for dinner, pull out the jar of *amba* from the fridge and start going at it with a pita. Amba is a fermented mango chutney of sorts. The main flavor, and smell, is a combination of cumin and fenugreek. Think of it as a pickled ketchup made from mangoes instead of tomatoes, except with a ton of spices. Okay, so it's not like ketchup at all. Store-bought amba is equally as delicious as the homemade kind.

MAKES 3 CUPS (720 ML)

INGREDIENTS

2 ripe mangos, cut into 1-inch (2.5-cm) pieces
2 tbsp (40 g) coarse kosher salt
1 cup (240 ml) canola oil
¼ cup (40 g) yellow mustard seeds
2 tbsp (13 g) cumin
2 tbsp (13 g) hot paprika
1 tbsp (8 g) fenugreek
1 tbsp (7 g) turmeric
6 cloves garlic
1 ½ tsp (8 g) citric acid
⅔ cup (160 ml) canola oil

METHOD

Toss the mangos and kosher salt together in a mixing bowl. Transfer the mango to a mason jar. Set in a sunny spot for 5 days making sure to release any gas from the jar once a day.

Once the fermentation process is complete, heat the canola oil, mustard seeds, cumin, paprika, fenugreek and turmeric over medium-high heat. Once the oil begins to sizzle, add the mangos and the accumulated juices and the garlic to the pan. Turn the heat down to low and simmer for 10 minutes, stirring occasionally. Let cool to room temperature.

Transfer the contents of the pan to a food processor and add the citric acid. Process and drizzle in the additional ⅔ cup (160 ml) oil while it's running. It should still be fairly chunky.

Transfer to a mason jar and set in the fridge.

DUKKAH

SEEDY SPICED CRUNCH

My grandma's nickname is Dukkah. Though it has nothing to do with this wonderful mixture of crushed seeds and spices, it's still a fun fact. *Dukkah* is made differently from place to place. It's just a great seeded, nutty topping. Use it on salads or roasted vegetables, chicken, on some labane toast. . . . The possibilities are endless.

MAKES ⅓ CUP (35 G)

INGREDIENTS

2 tbsp (18 g) pine nuts
1 tbsp (8 g) pumpkin seeds
1 tbsp (9 g) sesame seeds
½ tsp fennel seeds

METHOD

Toast the pine nuts and pumpkin seeds in a dry pan over medium heat, tossing, for about a minute until fragrant. Transfer to a mortar.

Repeat with the sesame seeds and fennel seeds for a minute and transfer the mortar.

Using the pestle, crush and grind the nuts and seeds until a coarse mixture forms.

Keep sealed in a jar or zip-top bag.

ACKNOWLEDGMENTS

Thank you to everyone at Page Street Publishing Co., especially to Will, Marissa, Meg P. and Meg B. who made this book happen. Without you guys, I would have never been able to believe that this cookbook was achievable. Thanks for believing in me! It's turned out better than I could have ever dreamed. I mean, look at it! It's freaking beautiful! Thank you.

Thank you to the readers of "I Will Not Eat Oysters." I am always incredibly happy to see you tagging photos of dishes you've made from the blog! Thank you for sharing my passion for cooking and food.

To my friends who allowed me to test recipes on them. Even when I failed, you graciously ate, nodding. *Cough* grilled-fish incident *cough*.

For all of the Moo employees that picked up the slack during this book's creation. "No . . . I don't think I can recipe-test that scone this month. . . . You do it."

None of this would have been possible without my family. I love you all so much. Thank you to my Safta Miryam who would never leave anything in the bowl to lick. Thank you for being my best friend and cooking me dinner every night when I spent the summer in Israel. Thank you to my Saba Haim for teaching me how to use a Sodastream and make the best piece of toast on earth. Thank you to Safta Tamar who taught me to always keep a kitchen towel over my shoulder. I wish I had a chance to learn more from you, but I am learning more and more about you through our family. Thank you to my Aunt Fanny who would organize a feast in a matter of minutes the moment she knew I was on my way to see her. Thank you to Vivis for helping and sharing my passion for pastrami and chicken liver. Thank you to my incredibly talented brother, Yoni, who is always there to make me laugh and ask me if I'm done with the Israeli salad so he can eat all the cucumbers from it. Thank you to my AAABBBAAA who taught me that passion and hard work will get you anything you want. For teaching me how to *eat like you mean it*, with no apologies. And also, how to take down a whole loaf of bread on my own. For being there, even at midnight, when I needed to know if something looked right and always knowing *exactly* what I meant. To my mom, I would not be who I am without you. Thank you for flying to Atlanta and back to be my sous chef on multiple occasions. For being my emotional, and sometimes physical, support. I've learned so much about what cooking means from you and how to feed others. Thank you for every phone conversation and text about fish *ktzitzot* and how to make it.

And thank you to my husband, Tassos. For pushing me through every single step to achieve and succeed in everything I want in life. For giving me the opportunity to do what I love, no matter what. For editing my awful writing and staying up late just to keep me company. I love you with every bit of myself and would not be here without you. Thank you, bubs.

ABOUT THE AUTHOR

Danielle is a chef, photographer and writer of the blog I Will Not Eat Oysters. She is an Israeli-Moroccan-Canadian-American, classically trained at the French Culinary Institute. She believes she was Korean in another life and eats with her mouth open.

INDEX